FOUR DISCUSSIONS
WITH W. R. BION

FOUR DISCUSSIONS
WITH W. R. BION

Wilfred R. Bion

THE HARRIS MELTZER TRUST

First published in 1978 by Clunie Press
for The Roland Harris Educational Trust
edited by Francesca Bion

New expanded edition published in 2018 by The Harris Meltzer Trust
60 New Caledonian Wharf
London SE16 7TW

Edited by Meg Harris Williams
Appendix 'Bion's model of the mind' by Meg Harris Williams

British Library Cataloguing in Publication Data
A C.I.P. for this book is available from the British Library

   ISBN 978 1 912567 60 7

Edited, designed and produced by The Bourne Studios
www.bournestudios.co.uk

Printed in Great Britain

www.harris-meltzer-trust.org.uk

CONTENTS

Wilfred Ruprecht Bion (1897–1979) was born in India in the days of the British Raj, and was sent to school in England at the age of eight. During the First World War he joined the Tank Corps and served in France where he was awarded the DSO. After the war he read History at Queen's College, Oxford, studied medicine at University College London, and then turned to psychoanalysis, to which he devoted the remaining fifty years of his life. He had analyses with John Rickman and then Melanie Klein. During the Second World War he and Rickman were in charge of the psychiatric rehabilitation wing at the Northfield military hospital. He was president of the British Psychoanalytical Society from 1962 to 1965 and moved to California in 1968, returning to England two months before his death in 1979.

Bion's books include: *Experiences in Groups* (1961), *Learning from Experience* (1962), *Elements of Psycho-analysis* (1963), *Transformations* (1965), *Second Thoughts* (1967),

Attention and Interpretation (1970). He also wrote the auto-biographical *A Memoir of the Future* (3 volumes, 1975–79), *The Long Week-End*, and *All My Sins Remembered*. In addition to many papers, there are several collections of his talks and seminars.

EDITOR'S NOTE from the first edition

These four two-hour discussions at the Veterans Administration Hospital, Brentwood, Los Angeles, took place during April 1976 at intervals of one week. The group, numbering approximately 25, was composed of psychiatric residents, psychotherapists and psychologists. This edited version represents about half the original transcription of recordings of the four meetings; repetitive passages have been deleted, together with material already published.

Francesca Bion

Adrian Williams

As a junior doctor in the 1970s specialising in psychiatry I attended two of Dr Bion's seminars at the Tavistock held not long before his death, and was struck by the electric atmosphere in the huge rooms overflowing with people and anticipation. Even the corridors and windowsills were occupied. Dr Bion, after a short introduction, solicited questions which were initially slow in coming but (moderated by Mattie Harris) they then crescendoed. He had a reputation for appearing not to answer the question that was asked; and at the time I often felt that his answers created frustration and feelings of inadequacy in the audience rather than clarification, despite what seemed to be his intention to stimulate further thought within the group.

However the four discussions edited by Mrs Bion in this book seem to me to be special and intimate communications owing to the clarity and focus of his responses to well-informed questions from people who had clearly studied the subject and were very curious and motivated. Although a very short volume, this book encapsulates the essence of his life's work, including his early work with groups and its potential application to the consulting-room situation. It is interesting that he was talking to a smallish group of about 25 medical residents (junior psychiatrists in the USA), psychologists and psychotherapists, and the discussions show how a work group was rapidly created, giving these four sessions a particular quality of progressive optimism.

Question: I should like to hear you talk about the theory of projective identification.

Bion: I don't think there is much to be said beyond Melanie Klein's version – what she called an omnipotent phantasy; a phantasy that a person can split off feelings, thoughts and ideas he does not want and evacuate them into another person, more particularly into the mother, and more particularly still at a primitive stage of existence, namely, at the breast itself. Of course the infant doesn't *do* anything; nothing happens. But the infant *feels* as if it could do that, and *feels* that it gets rid of some characteristic which it doesn't like and then becomes afraid that that same characteristic is directed toward it by the other person – originally by the mother, or by the breast into which it projects it. The theory was not intended as a substitute for already existing psychoanalytic theories, but as an addition to them.

Question: You have used the term 'bizarre bits' to describe one aspect of projective identification. Could you elaborate on that?

Bion: I never intended it to be a technical term, but in discussing it with Melanie Klein I suggested that these bits which are supposed to be projected, these parts of oneself which one doesn't like, then become bits which are felt to exist, as it were, outside oneself. I think that would help to explain certain types of behaviour.

We talk about 'getting back' to childhood or infancy. It is a useful phrase, but I think it is meaningless. Do any of us 'get back' to infancy or childhood, or even tomorrow? It is clear that we don't. Why do we bother to talk about these things which, supposedly, have their origin very early in one's life? What if we do develop a character in infancy or childhood'? What does it matter? Why any sort of psychoanalytic approach? The answer seems to be, and it also seems – how justifiably is another matter – to be worthwhile bringing to light some of these alleged early developments. We could say that these characteristics which are supposedly split off, or got rid of in some way, are forgotten – and after all, we do not continue to behave like infants; apparently these things *are* got rid of. Do you remember when you were at the breast? No, it's forgotten or got rid of. But having been forgotten these things persist in some archaic way in one's mind, so that they still continue to operate, to make themselves felt. We are not aware of them although other people may be. Since they operate in this archaic way they go on affecting one's work. That is why it is supposed that the analyst has to be as thoroughly analysed as possible.

Question: When you talk about being thoroughly analysed, are you referring to bringing those things up to consciousness? What effect does a deep interpretation have – like that regarding the breast relationship?

Bion: The immediate reaction, from my experience, is that it is so much nonsense – a foible of the analyst. I cannot see what other preliminary reaction there can be. But after a time you begin to think there may be something in it and to be suspicious that you do behave in this peculiar manner and that therefore there is much to be said for that theoretical formulation. But to speak of a theory as if it were 'absolute truth' is ridiculous. Luckily most of us react negatively to that kind of dogmatic statement and seem to preserve our own view. The problem is how to make a statement decisively and clearly in such a way that it is possible for the other person to understand it.

Supposing there is some truth in this idea that the event is forgotten and then operates in this archaic manner, what does the individual do about it? All *I* can do is draw the patient's conscious attention to a view which, as likely as not, they regard as one of these things which psychoanalysts say. But if that was all there was to it, it would just stop there. We must assume that these ideas seep through; the individual is able to communicate with himself. Look at it another way: Why does the individual say he hates or fears the analyst? That is a feeling and if the patient says that, I haven't much doubt that he says it because he means it. If that patient has that feeling, how does that feeling seep up into consciousness to a point where it can be articulated? There must be some method of communication between these forgotten things and the conscious ability of the individual to articulate them. An infant could feel terrified or angry or hostile, but would have no language with which to express it other than by a tantrum or a rage. In analysis it appears to be possible for people to communicate fear or hostility, or love or affection to themselves and then translate it into articulate speech – if possible even the kind of language they think the analyst understands.

To turn to another point: is a psychoanalysis that goes on for two years, three years, four years, five times a week ad infinitum, the only approach? One hopes not. But at the same time, I haven't come across anything which is more effective, and I am sufficiently convinced of its effectiveness to want to persist in it. It is, however, dangerous to be satisfied with psychoanalysis itself; a psychoanalyst must be dissatisfied with psychoanalysis. But we all hate the upheaval of revising our views; it is so disturbing to think that we might change in such a way as to feel compelled to change our partner or profession or country or society. Thus the pressure to say 'thus far and no further' sets up a resistance to learning.

Question: Confronted with a world in which all established standards have collapsed man realises with a sudden surge of despair that he no longer has recourse to any higher appeal. This means that he is totally free but has what Camus and Sade call 'dreadful freedom'; man must now assume the responsibility for all of his actions with no appeal to a supreme authority. 'There are no longer guilty men' says Camus, 'but only responsible ones.' In existential thinking this has several implications. Unable to stand the anguish of uncertainty a man may lapse back into some readymade pattern of behaviour, letting himself fall into a stereotype – religious;

political, philosophical and so on. Camus calls it 'philosophical suicide'. Or a man may make a leap into faith by creating for himself a new deity as a transcendent source of appeal. My question is: When you are confronted with a patient who is vacillating between coming to terms with himself, learning to be introspective, and falling back on the quasi-religion, whether it is psychoanalysis or standard religion, how would you feel about guiding that person to self-realisation?

Bion: I have an objection to guiding the person, because I cannot believe that I know how to conduct my own life. Many years of experience indicate to me that I am still in existence more by luck than judgement – that is the only way I can put it. Therefore, I dislike suggesting to somebody else how they should solve a problem. Of course, patients ask you to do that for them, and of course you always are doing it for them – even if unwittingly – because the fact that one turns up in the office so many days a week and expects the patient to do the same, itself suggest that that is the way to behave. And because I behave, or try to behave in a particular way in analysis, the patient – like the child who is fascinated by the bad habits of the parent – is most likely to pick up our bad habits, not our good ones. It is possible that patients convert them into some sort of symptom which they then repeat until they get it right themselves they solve the problem. A patient may learn the particular habit or mannerism – such as I have with my hands for example – but if they pick it up and repeat it. it begins to feel wrong to them; they feel that it doesn't suit *them* and seem to correct it in some way. It is not always the case; the psychotic patient pays little attention to a communication unless it is on exactly the right wavelength. He is very precise, very exact and does not like interpretations which are off the beam; he usually ignores them as if they haven't been said at all.

Question: If analysis enables the patient to learn to articulate early, forgotten or put-aside memories, how does that lead to change?

Bion: It appears to be because it is articulated, but I don't think it is true. I would prefer to say that this habit of grunting and making noises is developed by certain animals – the human animal being the most striking example – into articulate speech. It is a recent invention developed over the last few thousand years, which is nothing at all on the scale I am talking about. The important point is not the patient's ability to express something articulately, but that if it has reached the level of the mind where the patient is relatively civilised, there can then be some interchange between this civilised individual, educated and articulate, and a primordial mind. This primordial mind I can pictorialise by taking as a model the fact that it is a survival of parts of our ancestry like the branchial cleft, signs of a kind of fish anatomy, or a vestigial tail.

Question: Is this similar to Jung's archetypes?

Bion: I think he was probably talking about the same thing. There exists some fundamental mind, something that seems to remain unaltered in us all. If the race develops sufficiently to be able to communicate in terms of articulate speech then it is only rational to assume that that is a total development. But it does not mean, therefore, that there is nothing to it except man's capacity to talk and his consequent ability to give himself the title of 'homo sapiens'.

Question: I have been thinking about this process of feelings 'seeping up' into consciousness. It seems it would often happen when the person is having a traumatic experience, like a loss or falling in love.

Bion: I have described 'emotional turbulence' as a state in which there is this kind of churning going on and all kinds of elements keep on obtruding – as in adolescence for example. (Latency likewise, but it is dealt with in a different way. The person becomes amenable, there are no particular signs of emotional life, because the emotional turbulence is, as it were, turned round; the superficial calm appears instead.) From time to time the individual is aware of this kind of turmoil and aware that there is some development which is striving to take place; the pressure which arises in a particular area is feared as being likely to break out and destroy his accepted method of behaviour. He will then mobilise assistance from other people, trying to get them into the system to help him suppress the forces which are pressing him from inside. The other people in turn then hate the forces which are pressuring them from outside.

Question: When the patient is in this state where he feels that he cannot handle these forces and tries to marshal outside forces to help, obviously one of the first persons he turns to will be you. How do you deal with that? Do you feel you should never handle these forces for him?

Bion: I try not to influence the patient into a way of life which might conceivably suit me, but would certainly not suit him that is a negative aspect of it. The more immediate aspect is that I would like to say to him, 'You are really expressing' – and then I say whatever I think my interpretation is. The object of that is to introduce the patient to the most important person he is ever likely to have dealings with, namely, himself. It sounds simple; in fact it is extremely difficult. One is always liable to affect the patient with one's own views, both those consciously held and others one is not consciously aware of the countertransference. The main object is to help the patient to be less frightened of his own horrible self – however horrible he thinks he is. The moral impulse is extremely primitive. You only have to look at a child and say, 'Ah!' in a reproving way, and you will see it wince guiltily before it knows any language whatsoever – or so one would think. The moral system, the conscience, cannot be appreciated unless its primitive nature is recognised. Unfortunately we have to use terms like 'superego' which immediately suggests something which is above everything else. It is much more likely to be underneath everything else, basic, fundamental. It is easy to find various methods of rationalising it, thus building up a whole rational moral system and a whole mental space for which we have no coordinate system as geographers have.

Question: You talk about the fundamental mind which I assume is something like a genetic mind, a mind that comes as part of our accoutrements at birth. When I consider a palaeontologist, someone who may search and search and occasionally find a fossil, and compare it with the process of therapy in which it is difficult to tell rocks from fossils, but easy to interpret many rocks as if they were fossils, I wonder how much damage we are doing when day after day with our patients we are hearing phantasies and assuming they represent some part of this genetic mind without really having the accurate tools to be able to tell what comes from the archaic mind and what is simply our own misinterpretation.

Bion: The disastrous nature of mental interference can only be excluded if it is claimed that psychoanalysis cannot possibly do harm.

We become aware of a mind, or think we do, and build this vast superstructure of theories without any real consideration of what a mind or a personality is. We learn these theories Freud's, Jung's, Klein's – and try to get them absolutely rigid so as to avoid having to do any more thinking. But we cannot make a conscious and deliberate attempt to help the process of development if we start by being mentally fossilised.

Question: Do you think morals primitive enough to be instincts? And if they are that primitive what purpose do they serve? Are they for the preservation of the person?

Bion: The persistence and survival of moral attitudes which may once have been valuable is often injurious. I can see, for example, that patriotism might be a characteristic which is valuable; I think it might be important at some stage of development to learn to be loyal to one's contemporaries. But I think you can get to a stage in which the formulation, possibly valuable at the time, becomes inappropriate if it persists beyond the period during which the formulation and its context matched. The persistence of such a morality can become dangerous. Think of the moral grounds on which people do things today; how easy it is to accuse somebody of upsetting the morals of the nation or the person or group. But we cannot discard these attitudes; the fact that they are primitive doesn't mean therefore that they are unjustifiable. The analytic investigation should display these qualities so that patients can make up their own minds about them and revise their opinions if they want to – not so that they should go on feeling exactly the same for ever and ever. Even if one has been an animal at some point it doesn't mean that one should continue to be an animal for ever. Nor, having achieved some sort of civilised status, should one therefore want to stamp out these animal characteristics. Consider genetic inheritance: anatomical and physiological theories seem to be fairly satisfactorily worked out. But are they also applicable to the mind? Does all generation take that same course which has a considerable body of theory attached to it when it comes to anatomy and physiology? Take a primitive form of life like that of the aphid, the greenfly; it is almost a louse and almost a plant. Its method of generation is incredible; it is one of these unbelievable facts. Whole generations are exclusively feminine; they continue to produce through parthenogenesis. At another stage the young have wings, giving rise to another generation which has no wings; and then there is the one solitary individual which is male.

Ought we not to be open-minded about the communication of ideas? It is clear that it cannot be done by one individual – our lives are too short. But the communication of these ideas from generation to generation seems to be important. The method of communication and creation in the mental role is something we have to be prepared to find is extremely complex and cannot be regarded as following the principles which seem to apply to physical generation.

We can do nothing whatever about the world in which we live; I can do nothing about the universe of not-me. But I *can* do something about me. In order to do so I have to make a choice – out of a vast mass of facts. But choosing what I am going to pay attention to also involves *not* choosing what I am *not* going to look at or talk about; in other words, inhibition. That process is, it seems to me, indistinguishable from the pathological mechanism of splitting.

Question: When you are listening to a patient, trying to determine what is relevant of what this person is telling you or trying to communicate with you, you suggested a kind of 'free-floating' attention –

Bion: – that is how Freud described it; as good an expression as I know –

Question: – treating it freshly as it comes and also waiting for a pattern to emerge – which to me implies something which slowly builds over a series of sessions, not one. Is there some way in which you can give us a feeling of how you work, of what you do in an hour or a series of hours? I am trying to get some sense of what it is you are looking for, what it is you do – or is that impossible?

Bion: I don't think I can do better than I have tried so far, but it does involve realising that you may learn something about me that I don't want you to know. I have to take that risk. You likewise have to take the risk of finding out something *you* don't want to know. The position of the analyst is somewhat prejudiced because the patient has already found out that you are a psychiatrist or psychoanalyst and from the outset regards you as an enemy butting into his private life. You cannot, after all, commit a bigger outrage than you do when you enter into, or seem to enter into, a person's mind. In surgery the fact that an outrageous assault is being made on the body is usually accepted, although you cannot rule out the possibility even there of someone taking very strong exception indeed to the surgical interference with their anatomy. A patient consulting a psychiatrist will want to know who this person is who is wanting to talk with him. The psychiatrist must be able to tolerate his extreme vulnerability; the fact that one lives to adulthood means that one must have done all sorts of things which would meet with disapproval if people knew about them – one is vulnerable. In a recent court case it was obvious that one of the attorneys decided it was a good plan to work on the weak spot of one of the psychiatrists. Your patient doesn't know if you are there to gather information which you propose to use against him, or whether you are there to be helpful. It is usually difficult for the patient to believe it is intended to be helpful it is easier for him to regard it as an outrage on his personality.

Question: It sounds almost as if we have an investment in coming up with an answer which encompasses everything we see so that we don't have to make that assault, so that we can give some distance to the person we are working with.

Bion: I think that is true: do what we can, we hate being ignorant – it is most unpleasant. So we have an investment in knowing the answer, or we are pressured from within to produce an answer and closure the discussion. Keats, in a letter to his brother, describes what he calls 'negative capability'. It is clear that he is talking about this same curious business in which most people want to closure off what they don't want to see or hear. That makes it difficult, of course, if you also *want* to say what you see and hear. It is one reason why it is such an extraordinary achievement that Shakespeare was able to be so verbal – he could verbally pictorialise things which most people don't want to see.

Question: If we assume that we can be open enough and fresh enough in a session to get some grasp on what is going on, really 'hear' it, and that we can get the patient to believe and to trust the purpose of the invasion is for their long-term benefit, how do we then go about using that?

Bion: It is supposed that having brought these things out onto the surface you can then forget them – because you cannot forget what you cannot remember. In fact it isn't so simple, because there are really felt to be some disagreeable experiences which are better not remembered. So this question about the therapeutic value of psychoanalytic investigation is far from settled. It doesn't seem, so far, to do any particular harm and there are people who appear to benefit from it. One could argue, philosophically, that it is a good thing for the patient to know who he is if he can bear to find that out, because if he knows who he is then he can have some idea about his capacities and potentialities. In physical medicine it seems to be accepted that it is reasonable to believe that the patient should live even if he is a murderer; not so in psychiatry. I don't think people would agree that it would be a good thing to make somebody into a really efficient blackguard. And yet, why not? If it is all right to mend a person's arm or leg, then why not mend his mind? Of course I could raise a personal objection to it; the first person the patient would be likely to try his skill on would be myself. In war this becomes crystal clear; you may have to deal with a wounded enemy who may start wounding you.

Question: Are you optimistic about what analysis may do to help people submit to this invasion, learning to trust the analyst in order to relieve the pain they find themselves in?

Bion: No, I am not optimistic about it. although I think that it is on the right lines. I do feel that in spite of the somewhat rudimentary nature of our approaches they are of the utmost importance. But is the growth of our wisdom likely to keep pace with our intelligence? – using 'intelligence' in the pejorative sense of the ability to learn tricks. It is a matter of the greatest possible urgency that the human animal should discover what sort of animal he is *before* he has blown himself off the earth. The monkey-trick department is far and away in advance of the rest.

Question: For the past couple of years we have been noticing here that when certain employees have upset states these are followed by illnesses – actual physical illnesses – and I have been wondering whether the illness was coming on before the upset state, or whether the body was signalling in the upset state, or was the upset state heralding a major illness?

Bion: The advantage of the physical illness is that it is almost respectable and it is relatively comprehensible, so that the person who has some kind of mental discomfort can welcome the physical ailment because that at least gets relatively rational attention. There is a pressure in the direction of escaping into what is already known – which may not be much, but it is something. These physical discoveries are made very early. For example, a child can be fascinated by the extraordinary behaviour of its penis which, if it is fingered by himself or nurse or anybody else, gets erect.

It's marvellous – it's a part of the body which seems to have a sense of humour, which cooperates and which is friendly. The child has a chance of establishing a friendly or workable relation with its own body which behaves as if it wasn't its own body anyway because it carries on in its own way. There are these peculiar zones of the body which do behave as if they had a brain or mind of their own. If we have to be clever about this and put it into anatomical or physiological terms we would have to say, has the parasympathetic got a brain? Does the thalamus do a parasympathetic sort of thinking? There are situations in which a patient shows great signs of fear; that patient may also have learnt *not* to show them. Such a patient will complain heartily of his blushing. '*Now* I'm blushing'; you look at him and he is as white as a sheet. What sort of blushing is that? *He* knows, because he has been able to mobilise this particular vocabulary. It would be foolish in a case like that simply to dismiss it on the grounds that the patient didn't know what he was talking about, or had got hold of the wrong end of the vocabulary. In fact one has to pay great attention to it. Similarly with a patient who says he is terrified and shows no signs of terror whatsoever; the terror may be so socially unacceptable, and to him too, that he tries to ignore its existence. I find it convenient to think of this as thalamic fear. I could say to the patient, 'This blushing you are talking about is something which is so painful to you that I think you are afraid you might kill yourself rather than have that experience.' But is it any good making a verbal approach? – remembering that this capacity to talk is a very late development.

In many of these cases one is invited by the patient to make reassuring noises. But then the patient once more realises that there is no hope of anybody ever understanding that his blushing is extremely painful, or that the fear is almost unbearable. We must be sufficiently aware of the curious way in which symptoms present themselves, as it were, by their absence, and avoid welcoming the patient who says, 'Oh well, there's nothing wrong with me. I'm all right.' They invite you to leave them alone they do not want you to intrude into their personality. Psychiatrists and psychoanalysts are indeed likely to become perceived more and more by the general public as a threat. Their approach to the mind or character or personality is felt to be something which could undermine government itself. People will readily say, 'It's all this horrible psychoanalytic nonsense – that's why people are behaving in such an unrestrained manner, sexual promiscuity and all kinds of things, goodbye to all decency'. That accusation will become more and more widespread as it becomes more and more obvious that psychiatrists are dealing with something that matters very much.

CHAPTER TWO

Question: I have been wondering why taking a history during an interview is important to me. I don't think I could give that up yet.

Bion: The first thing you have to consider is yourself and your way of working. If it is convenient to you to start off in some particular way you should do so. You can readjust it if you run up against a case in which it seems unsuitable. Patients are often used to this routine of giving a history, and you may as well let them feel at home by allowing them to do exactly that – otherwise it is so strange to them. If you start off by saying, 'Now, what do you want?' or 'What can I do for you?', the patient may reply, 'That's what I came here to find out', and will not move from that point. You are straight away in the middle of a story without knowing anything of its beginning. The essential thing is to give patients as much help in that way as you can, because they are the people who don't know what they are up to. If it can ease the situation for them to follow the sort of routine they are used to that's a good idea.

Question: I would like to get a concrete idea of how you personally work with patients, to what extent you guide the direction of a patient's introspection and talk as opposed to letting the patient talk about what he or she wishes.

Bion: I would like to be able to say that I don't guide them, but in fact that is not true. It is a great mistake for an analyst to imagine that he doesn't. Theoretically you leave patients plenty of space to say whatever they like, but in fact your mere presence distorts the whole picture. They take one look at you and make up their minds either that they are prepared to talk to you, or that under no circumstances will they do so. The relationship between the two people is a two-way affair and in so far as one is concerned with demonstrating that relationship it is not a matter of talking about analyst and analysand; it is talking about something *between* the two of them.

Question: Most people talk about personality or mind as if it were located in a person. It seems to me that the only sensible way to think about personality is to talk about a functional relationship.

Bion: What I have just been saying about the patient applies also to the analyst; the physical presence of somebody else in the room dominates his ideas. You can see the person; you can hear the person; therefore you are powerfully stimulated by your senses. We believe there is a character or personality which has the same sort of boundaries as the physical body which can be seen and heard. Why does one suppose that there is some kind of mental phenomenon? If you watch any group of people – a crowd at a football match for example – you get the impression that there is more to it than just the physical presence of those people; there is some sort of communication that is not visible. It is audible because of the cheers or shouting – there is a verbal expression. But it is a verbal expression by something which is not sensuously perceivable.

Question: Although I have entertained ideas of the sort you are mentioning. I find myself afraid in the therapy session to act as if they were true. I think my fear is that I would be behaving much more crazily than the patient ever could.

Bion: I think you are right. If one assumes that there is a mind, then the question arises, what sort of mind? Terms like 'crazy' are widely used – one wonders why. Can there be this widely accepted word unless it is about something? And if it is about human beings, as it always is, it is difficult to imagine that one is somehow exempted from exactly that same situation. So I think it is only right to assume that if it is fair to talk about people being crazy or sensible, then it must be true of all human beings. It would be foolish to imagine that one is *ex officio* sane or sensible and that other people are not.

Question: I am not sure that I see how that follows. Certainly the word 'blonde' applies to human beings, and yet some human beings are blonde and some are not. I may agree with the conclusion. but I am not sure that I know how you are getting there from the notion that since the word 'crazy' applies to human beings. then it must apply to all human beings.

Bion: Because it is so universally applied, such a commonplace, one of these words which are used over and over again. I don't know enough about foreign languages to know how widely spread it is; certainly there are some words which have a universal currency. But I don't think linguistics would get us very far – we, as analysts, have gone beyond that point already.

Question: How does this and the things we have been talking about relate to what you actually do behaviourally in working with somebody who is your client?

Bion: That question is a difficult one which has, in a way, been vitiated already because there are such masses of ideas about what we do. In fact when you and the patient are seated in a room together, that is a unique situation – if we are right in supposing that we need to respect the peculiarity, the speciality of a particular relationship. An individual comes to see me; he thinks I am a psychoanalyst; I think he is a patient. In fact I don't know. What would you do? Would you talk, pass the time of day? Closeted in a room, alone with a strange person, you have to decide in a flash how you will behave. When the patient comes into the room you have to make up your mind there and then, with very little information to go upon, what you will do. At that point I think one is justified in falling back on theories. In physical medicine you are supposed to be able to observe the difference between a patient who has a cachectic flush and one who has ordinary sunburn. A good physician will walk into a ward and will notice that somebody is extremely ill, or somebody is showing other signs which obtrude themselves on his perception. In analysis the same thing applies; we are supposed to be able to notice some quality which makes us think that one particular person isn't another particular person. For about three sessions the whole of psychoanalysis is very useful – that is all you have to fall back on anyway since you know nothing else. But it is only useful because it might enable you to say something appropriate to the person concerned, passing the time until you know who you are talking to.

Question: I am curious to know what you regard as generally appropriate behaviour for a therapist.

Bion: My reaction to that is that you cannot say what is appropriate and what is not. Fundamentally there is nothing that you can do about it – if you can, then it is wrong. What patients have to realise is that they have to put up with having me there. It is useless my wanting to give the impression that they are dealing with a doctor or analyst; I have to dare to be alone in the room with someone who can have his own opinion about who I am. This may not be at all the sort of opinion I would like, so it is a matter of not minding that situation. One of the advantages of having an analysis is that you get used to the fact that your analyst makes comments about who you are, so that by the time you yourself are treating people you may be more able to tolerate that situation.

Question: Patients will often verbalise that they want to know who you are or know something about you. I had a patient last week who was very keen that I call her by her first name, very upset that I would not. She had just seen another therapist who had been recommended to her and she was quick to point out that he had called her by her first name. She asked why I didn't. She felt estranged from me – if I cared about her I would call her by her first name. She said, 'The only people who call me by my last name are bill collectors.' How do you deal with that?

Bion: It is difficult to say because I wasn't there. I might have said to the patient, 'I think you must be very afraid of what I would call you if I were honest. You are anxious that I should diagnose you as Mary Smith or whatever. You don't mind if I call you by a particular name of your choice, but you are afraid of what the words would be that I would use if I were honest.' But I don't know the patient nor whether she could stand that.

Question: She could stand it. She feels she is a whore; this is what her father has implied. She says, 'Because I have sexual desires for more than one man, my father must be right'. She is having an affair with another man; she is married and has children. In some ways she wants to be closer to me at this particular point. She wouldn't be put off by what you suggest; she would get irritated with your reply and insist that you call her by her first name.

Bion: Why not the second one? Why not whore? Or prostitute? If she isn't one, then what's the trouble? Is she wanting to be called a prostitute or a whore? If not, what is the point of the story? What convinced her that her father was right?

Question: She wants sex with other men besides her husband, therefore in her view she must be a whore. She's afraid that if she got a divorce from her husband she would run around and have sex with all sorts of men – behave like a free whore.

Bion: In view of what you are saying I think I would try to draw her attention to the way in which she wishes to limit my freedom about what I call her. It is just as much a limitation if the patient wants you to give the correct interpretation. Why shouldn't I be free to form my own opinion that she's a whore, or that she is something quite different? Why be angry with me because in fact I am free to come to my own conclusions?

Question: Her fear is that your own conclusion will be that she is a whore.

Bion: But why shouldn't I be allowed to come to that conclusion?

Question: So you conclude she is a whore – now where are you?

Bion: But I haven't said that I do. The point I want to show is that there is a wish to limit my freedom of thought To exaggerate it for the sake of clarity. It is ridiculous for a patient to come to see a doctor and say, 'Doctor, I've got a lump in my breast. Now, I don't want to hear anything about cancer or anything of that kind.' Is the patient coming for a diagnosis? If not, what is she coming for? It is not fundamentally different if the patient wants to lay down the law beforehand about what you are to think or feel about her.

Question: I gather there are basically two trains in your thinking. One is that you are primarily interested in interaction between you and the person in the room – not too interested in what takes place outside the room. The second is that you are primarily interested in noticing patterns of this person's behaviour; you seem to be asking not *why* the person is this way, but *what* and *how*.

Bion: Although I would like to have knowledge, from whatever source, about the person, my justification for sticking to what I can see and hear for myself is that experience – which is not simply experience of psychoanalysis – has persuaded me that hearsay evidence is extremely unreliable. It is frightening to feel one is limited to what one can observe for oneself, because you learn the fallibility of your own senses. But at least if you can see and hear for yourself you can have a certain amount of evidence for what you are saying.

Question: Would you discount, therefore, the fact that the girl's father called her a whore? Would you try to find out if she were a whore, or if she thought of herself as a whore?

Bion: No. I think I would feel that it told me more about the father than about the daughter. This is one of the snags about an interpretation. The patient may not know much about me or psychoanalysis, but my interpretation will tell him more about who I am than about who he is. I hope it will tell him something about who he is, but even if he feels that what I say *is* right the fact that *I* say so tells him something about me.

Question: What is the advantage of that?

Bion: There seems to me to be a great deal of value in respecting the facts. Therefore the patient needs to have some respect for what they see the facts to be.

Question: You've got me puzzled. I can readily see this in terms of some of the research into psychoanalysis and psychotherapy, saying that the patient adopts a relationship with the therapist and in a sense imitates or incorporates aspects of the therapist's personality. But I don't see the facts, because the impression I am getting from you is that interpretation in conversation is basically to keep the meetings going so that something like black magic takes place and the patient changes his behaviour based on the incorporation of the strong ego or good ego of the therapist. We do know that some therapists live rather wild lives and their patients end up having wild lives. Some therapists are rather conventional and their patients end up being rather conventional. So I wonder if it is the facts, or just a technique by which you can keep the relationship going until something magic takes place.

Bion: Here again I shall have to fall back on theory which is a sort of summary of my experience. The human being is what I would call extremely clever. There are certain animals which are clever – circus-trained animals, for example, can behave exactly like a Lord Mayor's procession. So you can be certain that the patient will be able to behave exactly like the analyst – and that is indeed what they learn to do. The patient only has to go on coming for a certain length of time to have a pretty good idea of the analyst's various foibles and habits. That patient can be *just like* the analyst and be cured *just like* the analyst. The trouble is that it doesn't seem to be adequate or satisfactory. It is the result most easily and quickly achieved; getting to a stage where the patient does not become just like the analyst, but becomes someone who is becoming somebody. is more difficult and somewhat frightening – it might mean becoming insane. Patients will, therefore, often prefer to fall back on being like the analyst. We can see how children quickly pick up the bad habits of the parents. The bad habits of the analyst will be reflected in his patients every time – very fast.

Question: Could you give us examples of the kind of bad habits you exhibit?

Bion: No, but my patients could. I can only hope that these characteristics will help rather than hinder the patient, that I am the sort of analyst who is less of a liability than an asset.

Question: When you are talking I have a sense that you are saying what doesn't happen rather than what does. For instance, you can't say specifically what the bad habits are because you are not aware of them; or when you give an interpretation it *is* more a reflection of the therapist and who he is rather than of the patient; or you talk about diagnosis of the patient in terms of what you are *not* looking at, or what you are *not* doing.

Bion: What I *am* looking at is what lies beyond the sensuously perceptible. Therefore you are quite right in saying I am talking about what sensuously *is not*.

Question: I notice in your conversations that rarely do you ask 'Why?' You ask 'What?' or 'How?' of the patient, and that reminds me of the kinds of basic patterns of human behaviour that Piaget or Levi-Strauss work for. I wonder if you are moving the same way.

Bion: Certainly; it is a basic, underlying pattern. One could go on interpreting *ad infinitum* matters which are of very little consequence or importance, but one would really like to interpret the fundamental thing. the fundamental language. In physical medicine this would be clear; you are not concerned only with what obviously presents itself for inspection. What you want to know is what lies *behind* that. Why is this patient not simply pale? Why do I think that this is a peculiar kind of flush? That is difficult enough in physical medicine; in the kind of thing we are talking about it seems to me to be infinitely worse. That is why I think it would be a good thing if we could consider in the course of ordinary life, ordinary experience, what this fundamental language is.

Question: Would you suggest a direct intervention to get at that level?

Bion: No, because owing to the cleverness of the individual he can always counter that; he can feel 'I don't want to hear there is anything wrong with me', and instantaneously responds by a defensive barrier so that the screen is drawn over again.

Question: How do you deal with it?

Bion: I don't know.

Question: But you do it, I know.

Bion: I think that one does sometimes. People do hope that the doctor will not be taken in and will find out what is the matter with them. I don't think people come to us because they have been told to – that may be a rational explanation of their rational behaviour. They themselves might be hard put to it to say why they come. Indeed one of the difficulties we have to deal with is a morality which has been forgotten and which we were probably never aware of anyhow. That is why, when a patient comes to see you, it is so difficult to know what sort of idea to have in mind. Rather than consider the situation as spaced in time – past, present and future – you would have to consider it more in terms of a military map in which it is all portrayed on a flat surface, linked up with various contours. This means that talking to a person it is all 'now', 'here and now.' Can you distinguish one part from another? And if so how would you do that? One way is to say to the patient, 'This has a very long history; these are feelings you had even as an infant before you could actually verbalise them.' I am doubtful about that method; the patient *may* be able to understand what I mean by that and to observe the characteristic to which I am trying to draw attention. But I don't know what sort of language is to be used. In the *Phaedo* Plato reports Socrates as talking about the ambiguity of verbal communication. He points out that the spoken word doesn't tell you anything more than a painted picture; it is as ambiguous because a painted picture has to be interpreted. In the space of two thousand years I don't see that any progress has been made with this problem. Occasionally a philosopher, like Kant, observes once again the ambiguity of language and the need that it should be made more precise and more exact. I am sorry to say that it seems to me that we, as psychiatrists and psychoanalysts, often behave as if it weren't a problem, as if we can do something with the language we talk even before having tidied it up.

Question: I think you are asking too much of man.

Bion: It is possible, but the fact that *I* ask it doesn't matter in the least.

Question: Suddenly, as you were talking, I remembered a story. I once worked with a man, and in the course of our conversation I said, 'The thing you should not do is go to college'; I gave him all the reasons – and he left. Two years later I was driving in a remote town in Arizona and stopped for a cup of coffee. Suddenly this same man came in, shook me by the hand and said, 'Thank you very much for talking to me.' 'What did I say that helped you?' I asked. 'You told me to go to college.' People don't listen. The role of the therapist is, in a sense, to be there, something like a blackboard. Maybe that is your key – maybe you are so busy puzzling out what the patterns of this person are that he has the chance to reflect upon things in your presence.

Bion: A lot depends on whether the patient can turn the experience to good account; I would like if possible to make it more likely that he could turn it to good account than bad. What matters is whether the person can have enough respect for the reality, for facts, to allow himself to observe them. I once worked with two surgeons, one of whom had a worldwide reputation, Wilfred Trotter, and the other who was locally well known and extremely proficient. If Trotter did a skin graft it took; if the other one did a skin graft, perfect in technical equipment, it sloughed off and was rejected. Wilfred Trotter, who wrote *The Instincts of the Herd in Peace and War*, always listened with intense respect to what the patient had to say; he never brushed patients aside as unimportant. He never even brushed them aside because they were so important. I saw him when he was called in to deal with royalty. He simply sat down on the bed and proceeded to listen to what the royal patient had to say. He said, 'Right, we'll fix it.' He then carried out what ought to have been done long before – a perfectly orthodox, simple rib resection. Nobody had ever been able to treat the royal ribs so disrespectfully before.

Question: I wonder if you are so busy trying to understand and listen to the patient that your comments are really designed to encourage the patient to keep talking so that you can observe him more.

Bion: Perhaps, but if you are lucky the patient may also feel that he could likewise dare to pay attention to such facts as exist – however unpleasant. That is the difficulty – facts don't make themselves acceptable to the human being. For all the laws of science there isn't any evidence that anybody or anything obeys those laws. It would be convenient if the world of reality kept within the bounds of our comprehension – but it doesn't and there is no reason why it should. That is why it is so important that we should have some respect for the facts; then somebody else might similarly dare to respect the facts again – it spreads.

Question: There is some controversy in psychoanalytic circles about the value of seeing the spouse or members of the family of a patient. With your concern for the facts and avoiding hearsay, I wonder if you could comment on that.

Bion: I have found that in certain situations I have been unable to avoid seeing the family. I prefer not, because I find that the amount I get, even from an apparently uncommunicative patient, is so vast that it is as much as I can cope with. If it suits you to see the entire family, then that in my opinion is what you should do. It is no good resorting to the method which suits somebody else. The fact that other people do differently is useful – it may give you a hint – but the fundamental point is, can you find out what suits *you?*

Question: You have talked about goals which you have in therapy, one of which is presenting patients with facts about them as you see them, the truth about themselves; the other is being available to them as a person. I am troubled about whether these are compatible.

Bion: Making yourself available is something which is more easily understood if you simply regard it as any other commercial advertisement. You must make it known that you exist, that you have a name and address. Who you are, what sort of person you are, is a matter of opinion which the analysand is free to form for himself. The analysand may be able to deduce who he is from the mirror which is presented to him – preferably without too much distortion–by the analyst's attempt to reflect back the meaning of his free associations. The analyst does not in fact tell the patient who he is, but leaves him to form his own opinion from the mirror which the analyst has tried to hold in front of him. It is a mistake to think that the analyst can tell the patient what his own character is; any such attempt would only be a distortion of the mirror. I do not think the fact of the analyst's personality is incompatible with the attempt to speak truly.

Question: You have talked about how, when you are with people, you are bombarded with a lot of information which is ambiguous and that what you are seeking is to find facts and truth. What do you mean by 'facts'?

Bion: I mean that I believe there is a fundamental reality even if I don't know what it is; that is what I would call a 'fact'. But we are prisoners of our senses. 'La réponse est le malheur de la question' [Blanchot] – the answer is the misfortune or disease of curiosity – it kills it. There is always a craving to slap in an answer *so* as to prevent any spread of the flood through the gap which exists. Experience brings it home to you that you can give what we call 'answers' but they are really space stoppers. It is a way of putting an end to curiosity – especially if you can succeed in believing the answer is *the* answer. Otherwise you widen the breach – this nasty hole where one hasn't any knowledge at all. In certain physical situations there are ways in which the hole can be blocked in a more or less convincing manner; if you are aware that you are hungry you can put food into your mouth and hope that will, as it were, shut you up; a mother can stuff her breast into the baby's mouth – if she does it with feelings of anger and hostility that is a different state of affairs from doing it with love or affection. Even in the domain of mental curiosity, of wanting to know something about the universe in which we live, that hole can be blocked by premature and precocious answers.

Question: Can the analyst guide the patient by expanding the space for curiosity when that seems to be the path for the patient, and by giving an interpretation or answer – not an omnipotent answer but one that might limit the space?

Bion: One would like it to be something like that. I am very doubtful that it is so because we cannot help sharing the itch of the patient to fill the gap. He wants to believe, and is likely to seize on any excuse to feel, that the analyst does know. And of course the analyst is quite happy to oblige. It is difficult to resist that; if you do you can equally choke off all curiosity – people think you are deliberately withholding information or knowledge.

Question: At Tavistock conferences they often say that 'the answer lies within the group'. They use this phrase over and over again. Upon examination it sounds at first as if it is definitive. that it means there is an answer and it is right here among us. And then upon closer examination it is infuriating because the search, this endless search around the group for the answer usually does not turn up an answer. I wonder if you would share a few thoughts on that theory – 'the answer lies in the group'.

Bion: I think it is a convenient idea because it restricts the area of search. If you were lucky there would be truth in it. The problem is, does the answer kill curiosity, or is it a prelude to an informed and disciplined curiosity? Any statement is valid as far as I am concerned if it is a prelude to the exercise of disciplined curiosity.

Question: Do you believe that a group has an unconscious?

Bion: I wouldn't want to abandon that idea; nor would I want it to obscure the discovery of what else the group has. It is easily done. I could say, since I have a body why not leave it at that? Why confuse the whole thing by supposing that I have a mind as well? We all know that the theory of conscious and unconscious has been quite productive; it may have been sufficiently productive to make us doubt its efficacy or use now. If you make a group approach. then it may become clear that this will have to be augmented with some further theory, because the existing one, valuable as it is, is nevertheless not good enough for that purpose. For some time now the law courts have been talking about 'rehabilitation'; they even call on people like us to express opinions, because they are aware that those time-honoured and experienced forms of treatment – guilty or not guilty, punishment or let them go free – are no longer good enough. So an open-ended curiosity is revealed; it is ever-expanding; the whole way of conducting our affairs is called in question.

Question: I am having problems putting together some words like 'clever', 'wise', 'intelligent'. You seem to me to say that we should have the common sense to listen to a basic language – that is my own interpretation.

Bion: Of course, in order to have common sense you have to have senses which work in common and that would seem to be fairly successful because it seems to happen anyway; the infant is able to coordinate what it hears and smells and sees. It is difficult to say how one achieves a certain common sense; it is easier to see that as we grow older our senses tend *not* to work in common. I was once an athlete; I couldn't be an athlete today because my physical functions aren't sufficiently coordinated. Presumably this applies also to one's common sense.

Question: So everything is ongoing and constantly changing?

Bion: I think so. This is why I have talked about 'turbulence'; I take the example of Leonardo's obsession with drawing water and hair. He could in that way skilfully 'draw a line' round that idea or feeling. In our work this turbulence sometimes becomes sufficiently obtrusive to be given a name; adolescence, for example. Does that answer anything? Is that one of these space-stoppers, so that you never enquire what has happened to that turbulence, why it is emerging just then, why it is that when you think you are talking to your little girl she turns out to be a young woman – *while* you are talking to her; why, when you think you are talking to this irresponsible little boy, he is in fact already a young father.

THREE

Question: Do you still do group work, or are you still interested in group work?

Bion: I am still interested in it, but I get very little chance to do it because I get so much pressure on me for individual analysis which I find extremely rewarding and interesting. Is anybody here taking groups?

Question: Yes; but I doubt the use of applying group relations methods to patient work. I don't think it works very well from what I can see of running a small group of hospitalised people.

Bion: You don't find it helpful with the actual family group?

Question: I don't feel ready to use it with families yet. I do get a sense of sub-groups forming and of groups getting into basic assumptions – I think family life is an established basic assumption, the pairing group in a sense. At present I find it difficult to deal with the complexity of the inner actions in my own life.

Bion: One thing which strikes me in dealing with the individual is how little consideration seems to be given to this question of what is basic, what is fundamental. Is there any way in physical medicine of defining what the fundamentals are? What does the doctor concern himself with? What could you call fundamental in the sense of wishing not to diffuse your observation or your time?

Question: I have often wished that in psychiatry there was something as fundamental as the vital signs – blood pressure, pulse. One can consider vital signs in psychosomatic medicine, and in psychiatry too I suppose, but it is much harder in working with groups or individuals in therapy to have something as a baseline of 'normality' as readily as the blood pressure, pulse, respiratory rate and temperature. I am not sure if that is what you are talking about when you say 'fundamentals'.

Bion: I think it is.

Question: Even more fundamental than that I suppose is that when in physical medicine a person presents himself to a physician and says, 'It hurts here'; if you look there you may find something in that vicinity and the patient is able to cooperate, to participate in helping you to identify at least some parameters, some areas where you might look for what hurts. But in the mental arena you may look in one place while the trouble is somewhere else. Most of the places the patient' points to are cover-ups – it is more respectable to point to the area in physical medicine.

Bion: We should not overestimate the importance of pain. Even in physical medicine some pains are extremely acute but not particularly important. Some parts of the body are extremely sensitive to pain, so if the intensity of pain were the only criterion one would be led astray.

Question: The intensity of the pain, or the area of the pain gets the attention of the helper the patient, therefore, participates more.

Bion: I agree. I am sure that it is important that one should regard pain as being a most informative symptom, but the intensity is often minimised or otherwise disguised. A patient says, 'terrified'; the analyst must distinguish a fundamental even when covered up by a cliché. Even in physical medicine of course one has to diagnose, 'interpret' that pain.

Question: I think we in the field of psychiatry have done more to try to interpret that pain. Our language has more descriptive terms developed for that.

Bion: Yes, but still shockingly inadequate. It is extraordinary, from our point of view, how little progress has been made in that respect – especially since we attach so much importance to verbal communication. It is difficult to know what is the fundamental function of language. Is it to communicate helpfully in the way a mother would want to communicate with her child? Or is it in the service of deception and lying and evasion? Deception and revelation are both fundamental activities. Taking your experience with children, what is your impression? How soon does the verbal communication become of importance to the child? And why?

Question: There is a variance in the time when children begin to develop language – possibly across socio-cultural levels. It would be important to know what is the social field. What are the acceptable sounds at a certain point? What are the social consequences of making a particular sound at a particular point? And what particular sounds does one make?

Bion: I am impressed by the fact that the physical birth is so impressive. The obstetrician's view, the gynaecologist's view, the statistician's view are all based on 'When were you born? Date? Time?' The *fact* of birth certainly impresses the individual and the group. But it seems to me that it is too limiting to assume that physical birth is as impressive as many people suppose it is. In physical medicine it is recognised that the prenatal history is of great importance.

Question: Do you feel this is important in clinical work with patients?

Bion: I think the lack of discussion of this point is a blind spot. Freud developed this idea of 'the impressive caesura of birth', of our being too impressed by it. He didn't investigate it deeply a great mistake from our point of view.

Question: In what way? How would you utilise it facing your patient on the couch? How do you use the trauma of his birth?

Bion: The first thing to do is to be aware of its existence. If there can be vestiges of what a surgeon would call 'branchial clefts'; if, in our development, we do indeed go through these peculiar stages of fishy ancestry, amphibian ancestry and so on, and it shows signs in our bodies, then why not in our minds? This is a purely academic thing we can talk about here; but what do we talk about, or think about, or observe when dealing with a grown man who comes to you with some complaint or another?

Question: Or a five-year-old child —

Bion: All right. Do you consider that the child is born on its birthday? Has the full-term foetus no character or personality?

Question: We had the very special experience of having a premature baby. I had a relationship with that child – born five weeks early – during the three days in the labour room before his delivery. I felt I knew his personality. The doctors kept coming in to take the foetal heartbeat to determine whether or not they were going to let him arrive naturally. He had a very strong heartbeat, although they were afraid they were going to have to do a caesarian section. But they didn't have to and I felt the strength of that child.

Bion: In a sense it would be possible wouldn't it, that the demands of physical medicine made it impossible to wait until the child was mentally ready to be born? One could say the time of birth was dictated by some critical situation which was not in accordance with what one would suppose was the natural development of the child.

Question: It was clear when he first arrived that he was not fully prepared. Compared with the second child, who was full term, his instincts weren't fully developed. He didn't nurse as well; it took a lot of coaxing before he was able to feed himself, to take the breast. Whereas the other one instinctively did. He had an immature liver so he was jaundiced and sick.

As you were talking I was thinking – I never put these things together before – that he was forced to be doing things mentally that he wasn't ready to do by facing the world five or six weeks early. That has been a characteristic of his behaviour ever since. He is mentally precocious now and always seems to be trying to do things several years ahead; his best friend is about five years older than he. I don't know if you can make a connection – never thought of that connection before.

Bion: We don't know. The point about discussing it like this is that we can mobilise the experience of everybody here and then perhaps be open to some sort of behaviour pattern which would be more understandable if one took into consideration the points you have been mentioning. I find it useful for myself to make a distinction between intelligence and wisdom.

Question: When you talk about the pre-natal period what are you thinking of?

Bion: I am thinking of it strictly in this sense of the period before physical birth, accepting the caesura as being of as much importance as it appears to be – simply for purposes of discussion. But whether it is as important as it appears to be from the physiological standpoint when it comes to the mind, is another story altogether. We have to use physical terms for this subject, borrow from physical language. I now feel – and I think that it seems to me to be borne out by experience I have had and am still having – that there is a lot to be said for considering that we are observing a symptom which will not be understood if it is supposed that it only develops *after* the child's birth. I wish it were possible to discuss these matters without having to invent a language as if it were scientifically accurate. But it is the best we can do until such time as it becomes possible to use it scientifically. It is useful to consider 'subthalamic' fear, meaning by that any of these emotions which have not risen to the point where they could be called 'conceptualised', or conscious, or verbalisable. Take, for example, the premature infant you were speaking about. What sort of mental life can you observe in that person? – assuming that you are dealing not with a premature baby, not a physiological object, but a premature mind. Or consider the auditory pits, or the optic pits. Embryologists have their views about what these extraordinary objects are, because experience shows that they appear ultimately to turn into ears and eyes. If pressure on the eyeball can make you think you can see light, then isn't it possible that pressure could create some similar effect on the foetus when it is living in a watery environment? When, from that point of view, is it able to 'see' or 'hear'?

Question: It has been found that the foetus can hear and responds to musical sounds.

Bion: Not the slightest doubt about it –

Question: The foetus moves in utero in response to certain tempos and responds to finger pressure.

Bion: I wonder when the psychiatrists and psychoanalysts will catch up with the foetus. When will *they* be able to hear or see these things? A very young child has no difficulty in observing, but its observations may be regarded as having less validity than the possibly less sensitive ones of the adult who may respond, 'Yes – come along, don't waste time like that.' The child obediently accepts the low estimate made of what it has sensed; it is suppressed and comes back as 'the return of the repressed. It doesn't come back into notice unless it becomes sufficiently dramatic; the grown person behaves in a way which seeps through to conceptual thinking and at last someone says, 'This person is hallucinated, deluded'. But that may be the survival of some kind of capacity for seeing and hearing things which the adult regards as insane or neurotic.

Question: How would you tie this in to your thinking or experience when actually working with a patient?

Bion: If possible you have to be open to impressions. Unfortunately the whole of our training seems to be at the sacrifice of our animal characteristics or our animal ability. I had a patient who didn't seem to pay the slightest attention to what I said, but was fascinated seeing my words going over him, and then thinking he saw them caught on the pattern of the curtains. I have also seen a very young child most amused at a frieze round the top of the wall of his room because those colours had a meaning which was comprehensible enough to make him laugh. The fully developed and possibly intelligent adult who sees jokes which we cannot is called 'crazy', or 'insane', or 'psychotic'. Are we right, or is this simply a lack of observation, a lack of being sensitive to the facts? Is it because one does not and cannot see what the patient can see – like those sounds going through the air and getting stuck on the curtains?

Question: Did the patient say he saw that, or was that your inference from the way he behaved?

Bion: That was my inference from the way that he behaved.

Question: What did you see or hear that enabled you to infer that?

Bion: I could see him watching in that sort of way; I could also observe that he had not the slightest idea of what I had said to him. He attached no importance to the ordinary – from my point of view – way of thinking or talking. The pattern of the sounds that I made was not of any consequence to him.

Question: Does something have to have meaning in order to give someone delight? For instance, the colours around the room which delighted the child.

Bion: I don't see why it should have meaning for anybody; meaning depends upon our interpreting these observed facts. In physical medicine you can say, 'Yes, the patient has a cachectic flush. That means ...', and then you launch off on your diagnosis. All that depends on interpreting the facts which are obvious to you, but first of all the facts have to be obvious. That is why clinical observation is so important. A precocious child can see and observe *and* attribute a meaning to what is seen and observed. What about a precocious foetus? Could that be said to attribute a meaning to what it hears and sees? If so, suppose the foetus could hear angry sounds. Would it be able to interpret them? Would it be able to attribute a meaning to them? And when you see that patient at twenty, thirty, forty, whatever age, are there certain meanings which that patient attributes to what is going on which would make you think that meaning would be comprehensible if I were talking to a foetus? The only reason it isn't comprehensible is because I am talking to an adult.

Question: Thinking in terms of what this would imply or mean when I am seeing patients from my clinical practice, it is hard for me to assimilate what kinds of things you attend to as facts. And what you use for making interpretations.

Bion: It is very difficult to explain, partly because the language we have to talk is so ambiguous. If I were demonstrating a patient's physical condition I could say, 'Look, that colouration of the skin there – it isn't just a bruise; it is something else; a symptom or sign of some underlying and more important – from a medical point of view – fact.' By discussing it here we may be able to become a bit more sensitive to what we see the moment we get into contact with actual patients. It requires a training which enables the physician, surgeon, psychiatrist, to denude himself of his preconceptions and be vulnerable to the facts. Knowing a great deal of medicine may be quite useful one assumes that it is – but what is much more important is that it should not be at the expense of one's senses. When we see or hear a patient we should at once be sensitive to what we see and hear, and from that point of 'observation' go on to the 'meaning'.

Question: You mentioned earlier the word 'reason'. Since the 17th century, when Hobson and Locke were much concerned with reason, most philosophers have agreed that there isn't such a thing; that what is reasonable to us may not be reasonable to someone in China or an aborigine. You said that to learn is to be completely open to the 'reason' or the modes of operation of human beings whatever their backgrounds may be. What kind of an approach, if there is such a thing besides a complete openness, can we as a group rely on to communicate? You stress the limitations of verbal communication, but there must be some basics that can transcend national origin, language and so forth, beyond just being completely receptive to the spoken word.

Bion: It is very difficult to say. It is brought home to all of us who have children whom we hope to educate. What are we to do? About the only thing that seems to be basic is not so much what we are to *do*, but what we are to *be*. That is why it is so important if the parents are capable of what I call passionate love. Then the child has a chance of learning something from the way the parents behave. Nothing in their school education or anywhere else can teach them this.

Question: I can see there is no cut-and-dried method of communicating, but I feel that the mother's love for the child, the nurturing love, the warmth, a hug or a kiss that is meant sincerely, is something that any human being could understand and feel. If a family were to give this to a child they would obviously have a far better chance than someone who didn't receive this kind of warmth.

Bion: It might perhaps help to explain something I mentioned earlier – the two superbly trained surgeons, one of whom had *become* something and the other who was just *like* a surgeon, but could never become one – not in this fundamental sense. It is most mysterious.

Question: This same phenomenon has been observed in different teachers. One can use all the media and follow all of the rules and do everything to perfection, but the children don't learn; another, by some mystery of being in the classroom with the students, succeeds in getting them to learn. I suppose it has something to do with relationship – caring about people and transmitting it in some language no one knows about yet.

Bion: In a crude way we can say one of them is ill and the other is not. But in fact we are dealing with something which is not pathological, something which requires a great sharpening of the senses and perceptions. Can we in any way find a method of excluding what is irrelevant and concentrating on what is fundamental?

Question: It seems as if that is really the dilemma that is being raised in these discussions. If I understand what you have been saying, you are pointing out that when we start out in the world, whether one looks at the point of birth or something prior to that as being the onset of mentation, we begin a process of responding in some cases with a great deal of painful subthalamic emotion to the chaos of all that there is to know and experience and feel about being alive; and then we immediately begin this process of attempting to categorise, to know, to find meaning – presumably to prevent some of the pain and maximise some of the comfort; and that in this process of categorisation you have to start excluding; and once you start excluding then you begin to lose the ability to perceive everything.

Bion: Yes – it's the dilemma of choice. You cannot be a responsible person who makes a choice without inhibiting what you don't choose to observe. You can carry this to a point where inhibition begins to slide into the spectrum of a pathological condition, inhibiting one's capacity to see or hear.

Question: Hysterical blindness would be an extreme example.

Bion: Yes; by that time it has become sufficiently noticeable, so to speak, to be given a label of its own.

Question: The psychotherapist hasn't quite reached that point yet!

Bion: Not yet, but later perhaps people will say, 'Well, all these hysterics take up psychoanalysis.' In a way that seems to me to be possible. Curiosity is so often linked with danger. The animal seems to smell out a danger because that is what it needs to know; that is one of the most primitive, long-range senses. For the human being it is very short-range. We can say a noise is getting too great or intolerable; there must be a similar way of sensing that a smell is too strong.

Question: The example you just mentioned brought something to my mind. In a combat situation we had Cambodian and Vietnamese scouts who could smell the nearness of the adversary and see signs which the Americans were incapable of seeing. But after two or three months the Americans were able to see and smell more because they had to train their senses for survival.

Bion: In certain intimate situations one would like to be able to communicate that – particularly of course to one's children. If only we could enable them to smell a danger or develop some sense which makes it possible to detect danger at long range.

Question: When you were talking about the patient who watched your words being caught on the curtain, I was wondering how you tested your hypothesis to find out if it was valid. What did you do with the information? How did you communicate with him?

Bion: First of all, it took me a long time to observe that fact. Indeed, this is one of the complaints made by patients – 'I come to you for analysis; nothing ever happens; I am just as bad as ever I was' – and unfortunately it is true that it takes a very long time before a point of this kind emerges. When it emerges sufficiently for me to be able to verbalise it I also have to consider whether it would be possible for the patient to verbalise it. He may ignore my interpretation either because it is wrong and just passes him by, or because it is correct and he doesn't like it. He can feel, 'This analyst is crazy' – a situation where the patient instantaneously projects his own feelings or fears of himself onto the analyst. Sooner or later we have to decide whether to give that interpretation or not. I gave the interpretation; the patient agreed with it and said he thought I would never be able to see the obvious – in fact he blamed me for taking such a terribly long time to say something which was so clear and so simple. On the whole that seemed to bear out that I was correct, rather more than it would do if the patient said, 'Yes' in complete agreement, but meaning nothing whatever; you know the patient is agreeing because that is the kind of thing he thinks you want him to do. These are matters of information. It is difficult to say why one 'yes' seems to be of greater significance than another – the fundamental ambiguity of language again. It is only a kind of elaboration of the grunts and noises made by an animal; we have learnt to be somewhat more expert in the use of our musculature.

Question: Could the patient make use of it in the sense of beginning to hear you more, beginning to assimilate some of the things you said?

Bion: There was a marked change in his behaviour after that. I can't remember now what it was, but at the time it convinced me that he was right; he had been saying this for a long time without any adequate response from me. When I did respond he was able to transform what I said in a way which made it possible for it to seep from conscious rational levels to other levels of mind.

Question: Isn't it because we not only make a sound to verbalise the interpretation, but it carries with it intonations, posturings that set up reactions and expectations such that the patient can now have this experience – which he would hitherto not have dared tell anybody in the world because no one would believe him – knowing that now someone believes him and that he is not going to be harmed for having the experience?

Bion: One assumes it must be something like that; the patient can become so used to having some statement of his dismissed as 'an hallucination', 'a delusion', that it is clear to him that the doctor regards him as crazy; he will not therefore make those communications.

Question: If the patient knows what he is doing and you know why he is doing it, why interpret what he is doing other than asking him why he is doing it?

Bion: This is another mystery. Why not pass it over directly from himself to himself ? Why is an external person necessary? Why can't the human being be like lumbricus? Why have a partner at all? Why not have a sexual life with oneself and no further bother? Why can't one have a relationship with oneself directly without the intervention of a sort of mental or physical midwife? It seems as if we need to be able to 'bounce off' another person, to have something which could reflect back what we say before it becomes comprehensible.

Question: It is an interesting fact that if you simply play back a vidcotape to a patient or a trainee without another person there to bounce off, it doesn't usually accomplish anything. If it does accomplish something it is negative. There is evidence to bear this out; patients tend to get worse when they are exposed to a videotape with no one else present.

Bion: That certainly points up the problem just mentioned: Why does the presence of a person matter? Why not just have a piece of machinery? If one could get near to being a dispassionate machine which simply reflected back what the patient says, I don't think the patient would get anything out of it at all. In fact, patients often try to assure themselves that you are capable of losing your temper and behaving badly. It is only when they find that you are capable of it – but don't do it – that it begins to mean something.

Question: Could you explain how the patient finds out that you are capable of losing your temper or behaving badly without your actually doing it?

Bion: I don't think I could, but I think the patient could, especially one who, as a method of trying to find out if you are really capable of being hostile or not, is extremely provocative for session after session, month after month. I don't think any patient is unaware of the analyst's ability to wear the correct 'uniform', the correct manners, the correct character, the correct qualifications – all that can simply be a cloak for the real person. Patients are not easily taken in by it – they may agree, they may feel capable of compromising as if to say, 'I know you are paid to talk like this and learn all this stuff; I'll agree that you are quite a decent fellow.' You enter into a collusive relationship. But the psychotic patient is somewhat exacting; an interpretation which is *approximately* right is not 'corrected' as a neurotic patient will do. A neurotic patient will help you, will allow you to be 'off the beam' and yet enable the beams to fuse.

Question: If the analyst's interpretation is not exact does the psychotic patient feel as if he were alone in the room?

Bion: The answer to that may depend on being able to differentiate one kind of psychotic patient from another. Some of these psychiatric diagnoses like the difference between 'schizophrenic' and 'manic-depressive' may refer to something which is so crude that it can actually be verbalised, conceptualised in this way. But these categories of diagnosis which are at present available to us are not good enough to deal with the subtleties of the situation you are talking about. In fact nothing short of continual observation is going to solve these problems.

Question: There is a notion that there is nothing more to psychotherapy than that the patient goes to a therapist whom he respects. not feeling much respect for himself that therapist communicates in some way over a long period of time his respect for the un-self-respecting patient who fights it every inch of the way, either by discrediting him so that he is less respectable, or discrediting whether or not he is truly respected, until finally the patient gives in, believes in the thera-pist's respect and ends up respecting himself. That's the grossest over-simplification one could come up with. What more do we know that could offset that as being the fundamental process?

Bion: The relationship with the analyst is only important as a *transitional* affair – it would be useful if the word 'transference' were used in this more poly-valent sense. Unfortunately patients can terminate the relationship because of one of these transitory cures. They get some relief and say, 'Well, thank God for that', and pack it up at that point. They have so little experi-ence of real relief that they are only too thankful to get anything at all and to call it a day – and to play on the fact that so is the analyst. 'Doctor, you're marvellous. I feel a new man – goodbye.' There you are – such a nice conclusion you might as well stop there.

Question: I have been thinking about your reference to answers being stop-gap measures in stifling curiosity and how difficult the resolution of the choices is when, as a parent for example, we give an answer like 'No, you can't', but still want to foster the environment where there is self-respect in continuing curiosity.

Bion: It is so difficult to see what is the equivalent of 'full term' in mental development. What is the moment at which the patient can safely leave, as it were, the analyst's inside? In analysis, or in ordinary medicine for that matter, the doctor can be very cautious. He can lay down rules; the patient *must* go on with the treatment; or *must* stay in hospital; or must *not* start work yet, and so on. That can be carried to extremes if the doctor is unwilling to run the risk of being responsible for a failure. So he can hinder the progress of the patient towards independence. But there must be a right moment for leaving hospital, or a right moment for leaving an analysis – being neither seduced into an early and premature termination, not frightened into continuing further.

Another problem arises if the patient is extremely unaggressive and fears doing anything we would call 'showing initiative'. This makes me think that the full-term foetus has something to do with the time of delivery; it can get so frightened of precipitating a catastrophic or disastrous event that it initiates nothing. Later on the patient learns how to be independent, but this fundamental fear becomes established as an archaic fear, something which is unconscious, something which is not known. Outwardly the person is brilliant, clever, so successful, so marvellous, until one day there is a disastrous outburst. The patient is alleged never to have shown the slightest signs of disturbance, so it is incomprehensible. There is no explanation for this extraordinary outburst which is particularly liable to take place at any of these times of 'turmoil' or 'turbulence'.

Bion: Seeing patients many times as we usually do, it is difficult to achieve that degree of naiveté in which we can see them each time as if we have never seen them before. It is easy to think, 'Oh, here's the same old stuff again – yesterday, the day before that, for weeks, months, years'. It cannot in fact be so because tomorrow the patient we saw yesterday, or last week, month, or year, will not be the same person. We should get as near as possible to feeling that it is the first time we have ever seen that patient. It is difficult because we always feel that we ought to know his history and so on and so forth – a backwash of our own medical training. It is useful for two or three sessions, but after that this information which one has from hearsay is unimportant. From that time on we should be launched out into a different realm altogether – not the realm of the patient's history.

Question: You are really saying that you don't have to take notes. Each time a person comes in he is a new person and it is only what is being presented at this moment that is important.

Bion: Yes. As I said before, Plato pointed out that language is extremely misleading – it appears to be precise and exact, but in fact it is no more exact than painting or drawing. A painting doesn't tell you anything – it has to be interpreted. Charcot, by whom Freud was impressed, said you have to go on looking at a patient until a pattern begins to obtrude. In physical medicine a doctor's sense of touch, smell and so on, should be so acute that he doesn't read books but reads people. With regard to these mental symptoms, what can we say? Neurotic? Psychotic? It doesn't tell us anything. The difference between people appears to be so striking that it seems to demand a description; so we resort to this crude division. We have to make the assumption that there is such a thing as a mind. I don't know what evidence there is for it – it may be completely erroneous. In Homeric times the mind was thought to be located in the phrenes – the diaphragm. It seems a sensible, scientific idea. It is obvious that if you start breathing deeply the diaphragm, working up and down, makes you breathe in and out. And if you see somebody else doing it you think, 'What's all this about? Is he trying to come at me to knock me out? What's he up to? What's all this panting about?' Then Democritus of Abdera began to suggest that the mind had something to do with this useless mass, the brain, for which no function had been found. The idea that there is a mind still persists, but we go further. Freud suggested that when a person 'forgets', the gap – the empty space of our ignorance – is so disliked that it is filled with bogus ideas, paramnesias. But since we know nothing about the mind, why isn't the whole of Freud's work an elaborate paramnesia constructed because he couldn't tolerate being ignorant of it? I am trying to get back to the basics – even questioning the existence of the mind itself. Once we are convinced that nothing short of such a supposition is going to meet this puzzling situation, then we can start making distinctions about what appears to be the behaviour of the mind. Supposing there is such a thing as a disturbed or disordered mind, where does the illness come from? What is the 'focus of infection'? Is it helpful or reasonable to borrow that term from physical medicine? Does it give us a clue? Most people learn to behave as if they are well. They find some way of training their bodies so that they can become athletes, surgeons. dentists, and consequently nobody notices there is anything wrong with them. What would we think if we knew someone carved holes in human beings – if we could not excuse the behaviour on the grounds that he was a surgeon? How odd it would look to see someone drilling holes in people's teeth – unless there was some 'rational' explanation. It is possible to find a rational explanation for anything, but in contrast to that it would be helpful if we could see what was irrational. Then it might become easier to understand why a successful surgeon who has done surgical operations for years suddenly has what we call a 'breakdown' and cannot face the operating theatre. Is it breakdown? Or break-up? Break-in? Or break-out? Or breakthrough? In other words, what direction is the person going in? Is the surgeon seeing something he has never allowed himself to see before

– how cruel, how brutal, how violent he is? Using the analogy of ordinary medicine. it is as if there were some focus of infection which has now begun to emerge into the skin. The mind, unfortunately, has no skin as far as we know, although Freud talked about the id, the ego and the super-ego – a crude, but shrewd subdivision of the mind into various parts.

Question: As you have been talking I have been going over and over a session I had today, and thinking that I had very little idea of what was going on. I would rather do anything than acknowledge that.

Bion: Yes – so would the patient, and so would we all. It is a basic characteristic which probably helps to explain why we know as much as we do today – it is so difficult to tolerate being ignorant, and so much easier to scrape up an answer which is a more or less rational explanation of our behaviour in order to justify our title of 'psychiatrist' or 'doctor'. I don't think there is anything particularly wrong with it except that it is a nuisance to oneself. The moment somebody comes into your office you at once feel the pressure on you to be the person who knows the answers.

I mentioned before a quotation of Maurice Blanchot, 'La réponse est le malheur de la question', which I could translate – again a matter of interpretation – 'The answer is the misfortune of the question.' Putting it into different terms once more: 'If you have any curiosity it is answers which put paid to it', or 'knowledge is the disease of igno-rance'. In any of these situations where you are in a tight corner you always want to find a way out – and that seems perfectly reasonable. When you don't know the answers – a desirable state of affairs if every session is to be an entirely fresh one – you have to find new words.

Question: If you think every session is fresh and new, why bother with history taking at all?

Bion: I don't. I have kept notes from time to time, but when 1 have looked at them later what do I see? 'Tuesday – !' What on earth is it all about? I have no idea. I should like to take a note which at least reminded me of something. So the first requirement is to be able to see, hear, smell, feel something to be reminded of – but what notation to use to write it down I don't know. If I were an artist I might draw or paint it. If I were a musician I might compose a musical work. But what are psychiatrists to do about it?

Question: Why do we want to be reminded? Why does it seem important over a period of time to be able to remember?

Bion: It is hard to know. The most impressionable years of your life are devoted to trying to forget what you are really like. You are helped in this – 'Don't do that', we say to the baby, and oddly enough the baby seems to understand. Don't do this. Don't do the other. Don't, don't, don't – that is the operative word. According to the psychoanalytic view there is some reason for remembering, but it goes against what has been learnt very thoroughly, at the most impressionable time of one's life. It may not be of the slightest importance that you wanted to suck your thumb some time in your life, but you can't forget anything which you can't remember. So before you can forget it, before you can discard it, you have to bring it up into consciousness again.

Question: Recently I have been thinking, reflecting after the analytic hour, sometimes during the hour, on how to direct the patient's attention simply to what he has said or the way he has said it. What are your thoughts about this?

Bion: In order to pick up these remarks, these signs of some mental, archaic element we have to be in a peculiar state of mind; the margin between being consciously awake, able to verbalise one's impressions, and being asleep, is extremely small. It is easy to be in a state of mind where you slip over into sleep, actually in the office when you are supposed to be working. It is equally easy to slip over into a state of being horribly intellectually awake. The border between the two, the correct state of mind, is very difficult to achieve one is always oscillating above and below it. Being on the right wavelength, which has to be experienced to be recognised, is unfortunately comparatively rare. Nevertheless most patients are able to put up with the rarity of it on the offchance that we may sometimes succeed.

Question: More and more pressure is being applied to the medical and mental health professions to provide evidence, to the various agencies that fund health care of quality, that there is some actual effect taking place from whatever we are doing for our patients or clients. Do you think we are ever going to reach the point where we can demonstrate in any objective way the effect of psychotherapy or psychoanalysis in the same way that people in other sciences are able to demonstrate effects.

Bion: I have great difficulty in believing that it will be so. It seems to me that the situation is so urgent that it is a matter of grave doubt as to whether we shall not destroy ourselves before we ever get there. We think we can formulate the correct diet for the human being's digestive system. I don't think anybody has got anywhere near to prescribing what the mind ought to be fed on. I know of no book on mental dietetics; I hope there won't be until somebody knows something about it. But usually the book comes first and people find out about it later on — the premature and precocious theory or cure.

Question: I seem to recall some books from the early part of this century, religious books on spiritual diets, mental hygiene, prescribing rigidly what people should think about from morning to night in order to be healthy.

Bion: Yes; the idea that there are things about which we might have second thoughts is felt to be repulsive.

Question: What do you think of Skinner's idea of setting up a whole community? From birth the child is taken over by the community?

Bion: If it is to serve as a method of watching and learning about the process of growth I would be in favour of that, but in so far as it involves imposing rules, it is like forming a shell which you then have to break through. We do form these shells anyway – and go on doing so. But the shell can become so thick, so strong, so powerful that the thing inside cannot develop. Any institution has this fault; any institution of human beings that I know of and of which I have some evidence could be regarded as dead. In so far as it is dead it is quite amenable to laws, by-laws, theories which are codified. These same institutions have inside them individuals who are not dead; they, the living objects, go on growing within the community which is rigid, dead, it obeys the laws of inanimate objects. The growth of these individuals inside the institution will sooner or later put pressure on it – it will start bulging out. Then the danger is a double one; either there is such a rebellion against law that the whole society becomes a lawless one, or it defends itself by becoming very rigid so that the growing individuals inside it cannot continue to live in that kind of dead institution. If this community of individuals is still alive then they increase the pressure on the institution which will then *have* to revise its laws or face disintegration.

Question: There is a community of people who are trying to be innovative, especially those in the arts. This incorporates a very large group, because I feel that it includes professions such as yours as well as music, plastic arts and so on. Disregarding the dilettantes within that grouping there are some who feel uncomfortable within the 'dead' rules, as you call them, and find themselves in the position of breaking out. Art is called anything from regression in the service of the ego, to various neuroses. Adler calls it 'compensatory theory of creativity', the production of art, science and so forth to compensate for one's inadequacies. The fear of death, of wanting to gain immortality and all these other clichés sound very clever, but under careful examination they don't hold up. I would be interested to know how you feel about that as a means of communication and its validity.

Bion: It would be helpful if it could be recognised that all these various disciplines – music, painting, psychoanalysis and so on *ad infinitum* – are indeed engaged on the same search for truth. Talking as we are here, we can split it up as I have just done; it is very useful for purposes of verbal communication. If all we wanted to do was to communicate verbally that would be fine. We could stop there we could say, if it can't be verbalised, out with it! Get rid of music; get rid of painting. But if you are tolerant then you have to see the possibility that the painter can make progress which is not possible for somebody who is capable of talking only one kind of language. The fundamental problem is, how soon can human beings reconcile themselves to the fact that the truth matters? We can believe whatever we please, but that doesn't mean that the universe is going to suit itself *to* our particular beliefs or our particular capacities. It is *we* who have to do something about that; *we* have to alter to a point where we can comprehend the universe in which we live. The trouble is that supposing we reach that point our feelings of fear or terror might be so great that we couldn't stand it. So the search for truth can be limited both by our lack of intelligence or wisdom, and by our emotional inheritance. The fear of knowing the truth can be so powerful that the doses of truth are lethal.

Question: You spoke earlier of the therapist missing cues given out by the patient. I have been thinking about the willingness of the therapist to be fooled or to escape this knowledge of what is about to happen. A lot of psychological autopsies have been done lately examining the actions of the patient, attempting to piece together what he has been doing or thinking. But I haven't seen any studies about the overwhelming fear that may have been operating in the therapist at the time. We want to feel that everything is all right and may therefore be looking the other way.

Bion: That's right: 'All is for the best in the best of all possible worlds' – Doctor Pangloss.

Question: Our fear may be just as great as the client's.

Bion: It certainly is. The only hope is that we may be capable of standing the stresses of it – nothing can demonstrate that except trying it. In analysis the important thing is not what the analyst or analysand can do, but what the *couple* can do. In marriage it doesn't matter how much the two individuals can do; there should be something the couple can do where the biological unit is two, not one. The two people who get together don't know anything whatever about marriage, nor about what sort of people they are going to turn into; it is another situation filled with the unknown. Can that marriage hold together long enough for the couple to learn a certain amount of wisdom? Analysis is an attempt to introduce something which is not so important, so fundamental as marriage but is an extension, shall we say, of playing games like 'fathers and mothers' which we hope has a value for the future.

Question: Could you talk about the three basic assumptions – dependency, pairing, fight-flight – in your group work.

Bion: They are crude constructions, generalisations. I think they have something in them because they are all basic, fundamental, primitive. For example, 'fight-flight' could almost be put in terms of the chemistry of adrenalin or glandular relationships; 'dependence' as that of the mouth on the breast and on sucking it. The general theory may be good enough for wide application, but in practice, in the world of reality, we are always up against the precise and particular instance, not the general. I am sick and tired of hearing psychoanalytic theories – if they don't remind me of real life they are no use to me. An application of a theory about dependence is no good to me unless it reminds me of something which I can see at any time in the world in which I live.

Question: I would like to hear more about what you call 'valency'.

Bion: That is borrowing a term from chemistry and physics. The relationship between two people would depend on their having various characteristics of which two or more came together – not the whole lot because there would then be no valency available for relationships with people other than themselves; that would be a marriage so perfect as to be absolutely unstimulating. There ought always to be some valencies left over available for attachment to something which hasn't happened yet. In a situation where we are simply Mr and Mrs Know-all there are no valencies – nothing to catch on to anything that is unknown.

Question: Does the patient come to us saying, 'Solve my problems'?

Bion: Of course; always this pressure on the analyst to know all the answers; always the pressure on the leader to know all the answers – which would seem to be the death of the community *if* it could be so. But that would carry with it revolt against the leader who knows everything and there would therefore be no chance for the exercise of curiosity. In the universe in which we live the opportunity for curiosity seems to be boundless – so much so that we try artificially to put a boundary round it. We try to stifle this curiosity by producing a boundless number of theories so as to be able to feel 'This far and no further.' Alternatively, there is a revival of thalamic fear – the fear which is so powerful that it makes thinking impossible.

An introduction to Bion's model of the mind

Meg Harris Williams

This appendix is a brief introduction to Bion's picture of the mind, its origins, and how it grows by receiving and developing thoughts, through the turbulent process which he calls 'catastrophic change'. And, in the reverse direction, how it retreats from growth and development. Psychoanalysis offers a distinctive method for engaging in this process, set in motion by the encounter between two minds, in a way which has vital links with art, science, philosophy and religion. Asked if there was a psychoanalytic way to the truth, Bion replied 'None whatever. Psychoanalysis is only a technical instrument, something we can make use of for any purpose we want ... to mislead or deceive people, and so on. It all depends on who is making use of it.'

Bion experimented with many metaphors in his attempt to convey his model of the mind and the way that the mind develops (or fails to develop); and he preferred to use his own terminology as he felt that existing psychoanalytic jargon was too 'saturated' with fixed meanings that could not expand to include new observed phenomena. However, essentially, his picture did not change over the years, even though its expression took various forms, from the mythical to the mathematical.

The mind, the body, and the self

Bion regarded formulations of the mind as inadequate – whether mind, self, personality, soul and supersoul, ego and id, etc. When asked what was the difference between 'mind' and 'personality' he replied, none: the problem was 'what to call the thing'. It is not the naming but the thing itself, the reality behind, that is important. He saw the mind as an apparatus for *receiving* thoughts not for *creating* them, and often asks us to view the personality as if spread out like a map, in a present-tense rather than a linear way.

In his view the mind is of very recent existence in evolutionary terms; he constantly stresses the mysteriousness of the mind and the fact that it is such a new acquisition that we still have hardly any idea what to do with it. We don't know what it is, where it is, whether it is bounded by the body of the individual, or indeed the body of a group of people, or whether it can seep through these boundaries and lodge elsewhere. He does however stress the inextricability of mind and body, whether we see this from a psycho-somatic or a soma-psychotic direction; and says that by 'self' he means the whole person, mind and body. He speculates that in biological terms the mind developed from the adrenal glands, and then attempts to process and digest thoughts on the lines of the digestive system. This supra-sensuous digestion is called 'thinking'.

Thinking is both tiring and frightening, and consequently we are liable to retreat into a mindless state relying on the artificial rules he called 'basic assumptions'. These create what he calls an 'exoskeleton' around the personality, which at first appears a safe protection but after a while results in the death of the mind as there is no room for growth. Instead, the personality should aim to grow outwards from within, on the model of an 'endoskeleton' – a mammal rather than a shellfish.

Origins

Bion inherited from Mrs Klein the conviction of the authenticity of the infant or young child's emotions and internal world before this becomes obscured by social and psychic coverings as the individual learns to fit into the community. (Not because childhood is an ideal or innocent time before 'shades of the prison house' impinge – a view no longer plausible after Klein – but because the child's feelings are *real*.) This infant emotionality underlies the phantasy life of adults and governs their mental orientation and its problems. Where Klein's theory was founded on clinical experience with young children, Bion's picture of the newborn or infant mind is primarily imaginative and speculative; but it is derived from experience in the consulting room that validates Klein's discoveries.

His speculations about the mind's origins extend (beyond Klein) into prenatal life and even further into the evolution of the human species, and they form the basis for his theory of thinking – of mental growth – and the negative forces that constrain or prevent growth.

Mental growth, he believes, requires a dialogue between these primitive and sophisticated parts of the mind; it is important that they should be able to hear or sense each other, just as it is important that the body and the mind should remember they are features of a single organism and need to understand each other's language. For the truth of an emotional experience cannot be approached from any one direction, certainly neither by somatic manifestations nor by deductive reasoning.

The growth-point at which two or more directions converge and focus he calls a 'caesura', adopting Freud's term for describing the trauma of birth. This caesura, Freud said, was 'impressive' but not perhaps as impressive as it seems, since if we look more closely we can see signs of continuity in the personality before and after birth, despite the radical change of environment. Bion develops this idea, imagining a dialogue between primitive parts of the personality that were nurtured in a soothing watery medium, and sophisticated parts that have adapted to a harsh gaseous medium and learned to propel this 'gas' out of their mouths in the form of 'articulate speech'. His analogy for the caesura or 'receiving-screen' where the dialogue takes place is the diaphragm, or 'contact barrier'; it both divides and links two areas of the mind, so ideally it should be 'permeable' not impenetrable.

These pre-natal, proto-mental experiences he calls 'happenings' or 'vestiges', like the anatomical vestiges of our 'fishy origins' that are found in our bodies. Bion suggests there may also be mental 'vestiges' that try to seep through the barrier or diaphragm of our post-natal minds. Mental 'happenings' are all unconscious and they go on whether we are conscious of them or not. They are indications of an idea that is trying to get through. In Bion's picture of the mind therefore, the distinction between conscious and unconscious becomes less important than it had been. It is super-seded by the distinction between post-natal and pre-natal parts of the self.

Mental vestiges of this primitive level of existence need to be unconsciously contacted, not because they are more valid, but because a linkage needs to be made with the primitive origins of a thought, in order to develop it further – there lies the source of its vitality. Many significant mental events are lost not because they have been repressed (which would mean they were once conscious) but because they have never made contact across the diaphragm with the post-natal personality; there was no way of hearing what the pre-natal self was trying to communicate. This results in stunted, blocked areas of non-growth, or in psychopathology. However this picture also implies that the blockage can be released and the mind can continue to develop; it is not restrained by bodily limitations.

Contact with these vital, archaic sources is especially feasible in dream-states (Klein's 'unconscious phan-tasy'); sleeping and waking states of mind also need to communicate.

The growth of thoughts and alignment with O

Bion speaks consistently of the germination, birth and growth of ideas. This he says is 'not a metaphor only';

it is a psychological 'fact'. A 'thought' or an 'idea' is an emotional experience that has been captured, linked up with, traced back to its vital origins. Such a thought represents the *truth* of an emotional experience and becomes a fundamental building-block of the mind. This kind of truth is not the same as Absolute Truth, which is of course unknowable, but it is related to it. Bion's denomination for this unknowable, noumenal world of ideas is 'O'. In line with many traditional philosophies, especially the eastern and the neoPlatonic, this idea or piece of truth enters into the world of the mind in a partial way, falsified for human consumption, at a certain moment and in a certain context.

Thoughts exist whether or not there is a thinker to receive them; they float around in the psychic atmosphere and are only caught when there is some kind of 'intersection' between O and earthly sensuous reality (such as happens in – for example – symbol-formation, or intimate relationships). Articulate speech is only one form of expression of a thought: indeed it is not necessary for a thought to be expressed at all; even if it remains unconscious it can still play its part in structuring the mind, through a process which Bion calls 'psyche-lodgement'.

Bion envisaged the growth of a thought as having many complicated stages, which indeed he attempted to map in a Grid. The Grid was intended to be useful in the consulting-room and he was not confident that it really worked; but the essential picture of the growth of a thought is that it progresses from something very small – a hint or feeling, possibly a wild conjecture – and then links up with something else (perhaps another mind, another perspective, an innate preconception) which enables it to take on sensuous form, to be 'born'.

Bion speaks of 'primordial ideas' or proto-ideas which may appear psychotic or even result in psychosis; indeed he came to some of his formulations about primitive thinking through working with psychotic and hallucinated patients. He then elaborated his picture of thought processes in the realisation that at first, all ideas appear monstrous or psychotic to the existing personality, because they bring the possibility of psychic change. Psychic change cannot occur without great disruption to the personality which would prefer to remain undisturbed, secure and comfortable in the degree of knowledge which it has already achieved. So an important feature of Bion's picture is this powerful resistance to hosting the thought, which is accompanied by what you might consider a type of pregnancy sickness. He calls the process of reception of the thought 'alignment' or 'at-one-ment' with O, the Platonic or mystical realm of the noumenal world of unknown and unknowable ideas.

Alignment with O is Bion's version of Mrs Klein's 'depressive position' – which entails overcoming infantile egocentricity, integrating split-off feelings and in this way acquiring the strength to have greater contact with reality (internal and external). Real strength is dependent on internal object relations. Where Klein considers the depressive position in terms of love and concern for the object; Bion in a related way but with a slightly different slant compares alignment-with-O to 'passionate love', a state of complex contradictory emotionality; and he emphasises its disturbing, turbulent quality, rather than either gratifying or peaceful qualities. Love, Hate, and the desire for Knowledge become closely linked and a strong tension is set up between them. He calls this 'suffering' and distinguishes it from 'pain' (which is associated with self-indulgence). This strong tension holds the personality in a 'paranoid-schizoid' state which he also describes as 'patience', until it is resolved into a 'depressive' state of acceptance and dependence on the object, and a pattern emerges. This state, although passive, is also extremely stressful; and Bion's favourite description of it is Keats's formulation of 'negative capability' – the capacity to be 'in uncertainties, mysteries, doubts, without any irritable reaching after fact and reason', which he said was the most essential quality of a 'man of achievement'.

Alignment with O is accompanied by a feeling almost of helplessness; Bion likes to quote Prince Andrei in *War and Peace* saying 'That is sooth; accept it.' It brings also a sense of aesthetic harmony, of 'confidence in seeing the truth', even though this does not last long: since as soon as one thought has been received, intimations of the next thought can be sensed on the mind's horizon. The sequence of thoughts follows in a logical progression; each one is built on the one before. The pattern is from ugly (confused) to harmonious (ordered): what once seemed monstrous can, when its true shape is visible, appear beautiful.

The apparent paradox in feeling both helpless and confident is owing to the relationship between self and object that is implied in 'seeing the truth' – seeing 'things invisible to mortal sight' (as he quotes from Milton). The personality is not seeing anything by itself, but with the help of its internal object or internal deity – a kind of personal O through which the Absolute O is mediated. The model for this intimate communication is the mother–baby relationship which he describes as container–contained. He uses the standard male–female symbols to indicate container–contained (it might be said these also have a similarity to the yin–yang combined symbol, with each side containing a part of the 'other'). On the basis of this primary link maternal 'reverie' comes into play, which is the process by which the mother receives the baby's emotional projections, meditates on them, and returns them to the baby in a meaningful state of order. Bion calls this meditative procedure 'alpha function'; it is predominantly unconscious as well as being of course pre-verbal (in the sense of articulate speech; though vocal music plays an important part).

Maternal reverie serves as a model for all thinking processes, since there are always 'mother' and 'baby' objects in the mind, and all thinking is a process of emotional digestion and ordering. The maternal containing object is, like the baby, in a state of learning from experience, not merely a position of authority. What is necessary for the baby's growth is not just containment, but identification with a growing mind: with the capacities and functions of the object, not just its understanding of the baby's distress and fear of dying. Bion, especially in his later writings, stresses the evolutionary aspect of O, saying we need both the 'restoration of god the mother' and 'the evolution of god the ineffable'. God the mother is the first object, the conceptual base, the first thinker; god the ineffable is the larger O, the principle of evolution itself, that can extend that first oneness beyond any knowledge contained by the first object alone.

This therefore is the foundation for the religious vertex of 'becoming', the type of intimate knowledge associated with deity or internal objects, similar to 'kyndely knowing' in the medieval work *Piers Plowman* for example – as distinct from the 'knowing about' which characterises the scientific vertex.

In summary: the essential principle of alignment with O is a very ancient one that over the millennia has taken many forms – from the hermit in meditation, through the mother–baby relation, to the artist struggling with symbol-formation in visual, musical or verbal media. It implies that we can tolerate a degree of not-knowing, of not being in control of our sources of knowledge. The process of alignment is continuous and never-ending, and means that the mind is oscillating constantly between paranoid-schizoid and depressive orientations, which Bion denotes by the formula $Ps \leftrightarrow D$. The mind may be almost immediately assaulted by new confusions but meanwhile it has grown, stamped by that momentary feeling of 'security' or aesthetic experience. The moment embodies the transcendent; but the mind is chained to its body rather than elevated beyond it; the personality is still 'itself', psyche and soma together.

Turbulence, catastrophic change, and becoming

As humans we are engaged in a continuous process of becoming, or trying to become, ourselves. It does not happen automatically but only through 'learning from experience' – a phrase which, as often with Bion, means the opposite of its usual conversational sense, and entails a structural alteration in the personality which he calls 'catastrophic change'.

For Bion's mind-picture is characterised by his stress on the difficulty of thinking, of learning from experience. This is perhaps a significant difference between alignment with O and the popular view of meditation as a relaxing anxiety-free state. Why is it so difficult? Because, he says, of the turbulence involved. Our default setting is to wish to preserve the status quo; we hate developing because it changes us. 'How can we stand it?' he asks, referring not just to the 'psychoanalytic pair' (as he calls the psychoanalyst and analysand) but to any thinking person. He is intensely aware that truly focusing on the experience of the present moment will increase stress, not decrease it – whether this is in the analytic consulting-room or outside in everyday life. The mind is in his view such a recent evolutionary feature that as humans, or mammals, we still regard it as an imposition and we would really prefer to go back to being dinosaurs, as evidenced by our constant attempts to destroy one another. Eating and being eaten are two ends of a single spectrum and it appears to be one that we understand. (Though terrorism – which he calls 'the prerogative of the mentally deficient' – is outside that spectrum, outside the survival instinct.)

Death by dinosaur mentality is one type of catastrophe – the catastrophe of oblivion, mental extinction. It is the opposite of 'catastrophic change', which is a necessary feature of the developing mind, and which Bion also calls 'transformations in O', because it indicates a transformation from learning *about* the mind to being or becoming oneself. The term 'catastrophic' is a kind of pun, with two alternative meanings: one being disaster, the other suggesting the moment of revelation in an ancient Greek play, the point at which all the misunderstandings and ambiguities become clarified and the hero finally accepts his death, a fate synonymous with self-knowledge. For in such situations, death is a metaphor for 'death to the existing state of mind' which in fact heralds a kind of 'rebirth' into the next state of mind, the next phase of coming to know ourselves.

So the first sign of an idea trying to emerge is a point of disturbance, of turbulence. It occurs at the caesura or diaphragm between primitive and sophisticated states of mind. Bion calls it a 'fact of feeling' because feelings are the nearest we can come to mental facts, and it is very difficult to observe them. An idea that is approaching some kind of intersection with O may be sensed by the personality with advance shockwaves, like indications of an earthquake. Whether it is caught or not, this new idea is liable to cause disturbance in the depths. In response to this disturbance, we have a choice: 'Kill it or investigate it.' Inhibiting the new idea, trying to prevent its birth, is in effect a type of murder; yet it happens all the time, owing to the exhausting and stressful nature of thinking.

The dynamic for the growth of thoughts is curiosity. Curiosity, by nature, disturbs the status quo; it can only operate in a state of not-knowing; it implies the mind is open to new possibilities, otherwise it cannot intersect with the floating idea and provide the soil for it to germinate. Bion believes it begins *in utero*, with propulsions in the amniotic fluid, creating primitive prototypes of splitting and projection. He expands the psychoanalytic concept of 'projective identification' to include the idea of primitive communication; there are different types of curiosity – not merely intrusive or controlling of the object, but also a vital link with it, without which thinking cannot progress. This communicative projective identification is what sets container–contained in operation between mother and baby. So curiosity may be dangerous; but so is lack of curiosity. The 'poor mammal' is caught between a rock and a hard place. Curiosity therefore is not just entertained but also suffered, in so far as it can lead to the turbulence associated with a potential step forward in development.

Metaphors and vertices

An idea is always caught in the link between two or more things – whether these be people, or emotions, or 'vertices' such as the traditional ones of science, art and religion: they are all different ways of looking at the same thing – the truth.

In line with this, for Bion, the process of locating and encapsulating an emotional situation so that it can be observed is made easier through the use of metaphors or analogies. He sometimes calls these 'transformations' or 'myths' because there is a central core that (following a mathematical metaphor) he calls the 'invariant' part – the basic feature that remains the same even when other aspects are different. These different aspects then throw light on each other. Extending this (with a chemical metaphor) he proposes that it is useful if a state of mind can be 'polyvalent', that is, open to making links with a number of other states, perspectives, or 'vertices'. It is easier if these different states can be imagined set out on a flat plane like a map, so they can be viewed simultaneously. Just as the mind is a group, so a group of people can catch between them an idea that is floating around in the atmosphere and its progress becomes evident as it tracks its way through the group. Thus a constructive or 'work group' can be an aid to observation. For this process of how an idea tracks or travels, whether or not it is visible, Bion uses the metaphor of Alpheus, the sacred river that runs underground (unseen) and then re-emerges in unexpected places: it is suddenly 'seen', but it has always existed.

Some of Bion's favourite metaphors for vision or observation are: the type of everyday blindness that reveals 'things invisible to mortal sight' (a quotation from Milton, but an idea that is traditional in religion and poetry); the sculpture whose impact lies in the spaces between, that trap light, so we have to look at the space surrounding the object as well as the solid object, in order to understand its meaning; the diamond-cutter who cuts the stone in such a way that it reveals a two-directional passage of light, a communication benefiting both ends of the spectrum, revealing inner beauty. He also uses astronomical metaphors, such as the giant radio telescope which scans the sky for minute specks of insight that might be lost in depths of preconceived knowledge. A mathematical metaphor is that of points which are 'conjugate complex', that is, they appear to be a single point but structurally they are in fact composed of separate points which have come together; this represents a meeting of vertices in harmony, aligning with the 'O' of a situation.

To represent the type of 'O' that is Absolute Beauty, he refers to the story of how Homer describes Helen of Troy, or rather, doesn't describe her: her presence is simply indicated by a movement on the city walls and we have to imagine her through a type of absence;

again, it is a traditional way of indicating that which is indescribable or ineffable, such as godhead or ultimate reality. What the poet shows us is not a particular woman but a principle of beauty beyond – pointing to the source of our awe and knowledge of beauty. In his *Memoir of the Future*, he speculates about a 'blush on the walls of the uterus' – again, the movement on the walls that marks invisibly the moment of genesis of a baby or an idea, of 'things invisible to mortal sight'. Bion says: 'These are verbal transformations of visual images. To some extent one can say one hears or sees the source of the stimulation; but I don't think it is true. I think you are always up against this problem of what *is* the source, what is the O, the origin. One can say "O" or one can cite the Buddhist prayer I suppose, or make these mathematical signs.' (He also refers to the Tao, the principle of the universe which is known by a sense of direction).

To represent the turbulent emotions which underlie the smooth surface of the latency or latency-type mental state, he uses the story of Palinurus, who failed to see the turbulent storm that was brewing beneath the smooth latency surface of the Mediterranean, and was hurled into the sea with his broken rudder. Bion finds latency a better metaphor than adolescence, since in adolescence the turbulence is 'too obvious' and what we need to do is to sharpen our perceptions to be able to notice the hidden and unacknowledged conflicts that lie beneath an apparently smooth surface life, and may dangerously erupt without warning.

Bion also uses metaphors from mankind's evolutionary history to describe our general difficulty in thinking: such as, the dinosaur being superseded by the mammal which finds it is equipped with not just a brain but also a mind; and the pre- and post-natal parts of the self which have such problems in communicating that come to a crisis at the caesura of birth; yet both of which are essential to the vitality of the mind.

Enemies of growth

The type of thinking or meditation described by Bion is, as we have seen, a turbulent, not a peaceful one; and the moments of aesthetic revelation are temporary, although he believes that even a few such moments are all that is needed for the mind to be able to develop. In Kleinian terms there is always an envious, self-destructive part of the personality; with Bion, the forces antagonistic to development are extended to the wish to maintain the status quo in order to avoid turbulence.

To take the concept of envy first. What is the envy of, exactly? Bion says that 'If the envy were to assume an aspect of whole object it could be seen as envy of the personality capable of maturation and of the object stimulating maturation' – that is, the envy is stirred by the growth process itself, and it is directed not simply at the object (or oedipally, at the internal parents), nor at the 'new baby' part of the family or the personality, but at the *link* between these objects. It is not envy of either container or contained, on their own; it is envy of the creative link between them (the 'symbiotic' link as he calls it) – that leads to 'gratitude' at the other end of the spectrum. Hence he says we should worry less about our inhibitions (the classical psychoanalytic formula), and worry more about our 'impulse to inhibit' this creative link.

The contrast to a symbiotic link is a parasitic link: when the two parts of the personality, self and object, get into a hostile or mutually destructive relationship. The hostile object is a pseudo-object; it has been constructed by the omnipotent self, and it is brought into action when the personality begins to move forwards, because it is envious essentially of growth and development. This idea of the personality's hostility to growth is an important part of Bion's vision and differentiates his picture from the Kleinian one (or indeed, from almost all other psychoanalytic models, which generally attribute failures of growth to environmental factors – with an admixture of constitutional). Bion attributes failure of growth to a natural dislike of having our minds developed: because it is always a process in which we are passive, not in control, and we do not know in which direction the mind will go or what shape it may take. Given this, however, some personalities have a stronger constitution than others, and can *tolerate* the growth process better.

So in Bion's vision we can appreciate how the personality is pulled forward almost, in a sense, against its will, by curiosity to know the truth or reality of things, and a sense of beauty. He constantly warns against the impulse to 'kill' curiosity, which is evidenced by sayings such as 'I know, I know' and 'I don't know' (meaning much the same thing: 'don't say any more!'). The death of curiosity occurs when a preconception mates with a memory to prevent catastrophic change: that is, the personality senses a developmental change is on the horizon, and quickly retreats back to some existing comfortable picture from the past (a memory), which will confirm its status quo. It is an example of the personality taking a 'wrong turning' which can happen at any stage in life, pre- or post-natal. This is why he advocates abandoning memory and desire: they are both forms of the same thing, namely, preconceived pictures, whether they are envisaged as occurring in the past or in the future. He doesn't mean abandon desire in the sense of strong emotion, but in the sense of a tyrannical wish to conform (or for somebody else to conform) to a particular image that is essentially narcissistic. It is the opposite of 'remembering' which is the process of making links to get at the meaning that lies beyond differences.

Hostility to growth can also take the form of lies which, Bion explains, are invented by the self, and may often seem to be very clever; they are designed to impress. This is by contrast with truth, which is experienced passively as coming from outside the self, mediated by internal objects. He points out that a lie can only come into existence if the personality has already glimpsed some intimation of the truth; this is because a lie is specifically a perversion of the truth – a covering-over through some kind of substitution. The creation of lies constitutes a Negative Grid opposed to the Grid for thinking. Though Bion did not actually develop the Negative Grid, he does speak of minus values of Love, Hate, and Knowledge (LHK). These negative links are not bad, nasty or painful emotions; they are *non*-emotions, an absence of true emotionality. As a result they may 'yield pleasure or pain but not meaning' or understanding.

When lies become systematised, they constitute 'morality': a fixed authoritarian system with behavioural rules and regulations, a kind of false ethics. All groups and societies have their own moral systems; and because the individual is also a group, he or she also has a personal moral system. He speaks of the 'outraged moral system' that impresses itself on the psychoanalyst who has become tired and confused and so seeks for some reliable explanation for whatever is going on in the consulting room (quite likely in collusion with the patient who may be pushing for some false but respectable interpretation). Some of these lies take the form of what Freud called 'paramnesias' (space-filling facts); some take the form of old theories that worked in the past; some take the form of an 'exoskeleton', a hard casing of established ideas that may once have served a useful protective function but then become so rigid there is no possibility of mental expansion, no 'room for growth'. Knowledge can be 'too thick for wisdom' to penetrate. Too much reliance on knowing-about does not allow for true intimate 'knowing' to take place through psyche-lodgement – when the germ of a new idea lodges in a 'roughness' in the smooth skull of existing knowledge.

Morality is thus the opposite, or rather the negative, of the passionate links of LHK in alignment with O. The idea of knowledge as power is a delusion and can be a manipulation (Bion regarded many forms of education in this light, and thought that true education was hard to come by.) Morality may have its uses but, for Bion, it is more important to keep an eye on its dangers. In his autobiographical *Memoir of the Future* morality appears in the form of a character called the Devil.

One specific type of morality is termed by Bion a 'basic assumption'. The concept of basic assumptions derived from his early work with groups, where he identified three typical forms of basic assumption: dependence, fight-flight, and pairing (or messianic). Dependence is dominated by a wish to find someone to provide security; fight-flight is the aggressive form of the same; and pairing involves a fantasy of producing a messiah who will save the group. Basic assumption groups employ what Bion calls the 'language of substitution' as opposed to the 'language of achievement'. They all constitute the avoidance of thinking for oneself and they are all are sanctioned by society; different societies may give them a different format to suit the prevailing moral system but the essential principle is the same – of demand for conformity. These groups operate in the individual mind as well as in a social context and we spend much of our time under the aegis of these automatic, 'protomental' states, otherwise daily life would be impossible. The main point here is to make a distinction between mental and protomental activity: one type of mindset is for intimate relationships, the other is for social convenience.

An offshoot from this is the concept of 'mindlessness', in which the struggle for object-relatedness is avoided or side-stepped but neither does it fall into an attacking mode. The term 'mindlessness' (implicit in Bion) was later adopted by Donald Meltzer to describe a special, non-aggressive mode of dismantling the dimensionality of the mind that is performed by autistic children.

Bion borrows the terms 'beta-elements' and 'bizarre elements' to indicate fragments of non-thought which have somehow failed to become processed into symbols through alpha function: that is, through relationship with an object. It is not clear whether he regarded these as proto-lies, tiny perversions of truth, or simply as the mind's rubbish – part of the massive amount of sensuous information that is of no immediate use and has to be evacuated. But what is clear is that the personality can attack itself, in order to avoid the turbulence of growth-pains. It is not just a matter of *telling* lies; the personality can also, he says, '*be* a lie'; constant lying-in-the-soul has a negative structural impact on the mind; it is not just a false front presented to public view.

The danger for the human animal is of being 'too intelligent to be wise'; he refers often to man's clever monkey-like tricks and the problem of technological inventions that are far in advance of our capacity to use them wisely.

The psychoanalytic pair

For Bion therefore, resistance is not to psychoanalytic interpretations (which is feels may often be justifiable) but to the growth process itself. Hostility is liable to be aroused by the psychoanalytic process precisely because it is an attempt to liberate or re-start a growth process which has got into difficulties. The aim is 'to introduce the patient to himself, which is a marriage that will last as long as he lives.'

So this introduction to self-knowledge takes the form of working as a pair, a 'work group' of two. Indeed Bion increasingly speaks of the 'psychoanalytic pair' rather than the psychoanalyst alone. The ultimate hope is that the patient will then internalise this work group and it will continue to function and develop within the individual mind. Bion is very much aware that psychoanalysis is simply one (very recent) method for this type of meditation; and says that self-analysis is a 'natural' function.

The work group is the opposite of a basic assumption group: it focuses not on authority and obedience but on the task of personality development. The method is based on the 'reverie' between mother and baby, the natural detoxification of infant fears that absorbs and processes them and presents them transformed to the infant with their meaning and understanding added. The prototypal anxiety (at root, the fear of death) becomes tolerable through being symbolised. Although Bion gives it the strange name of 'alpha function' it is a natural process, and the model for the psychoanalytical relationship. The psychoanalytic pair work on an analogous basis: as the meaning of anxiety takes shape, it loses its destructiveness and becomes absorbed into the structure of the mind in the form of self-knowledge. As in ordinary personality development, there is a continuous oscillation between Ps (paranoid-schizoid) and D (depressive) positions: anxiety (requiring patience and suffering) and security or harmony (the sense of being understood, of being in line with O).

Something that Bion hints at from early on and makes clearer in his late talks, is that the analysis, rather than the analyst, is the true container for this turbulent oscillation between Ps and D. 'The personality has a container–contained relationship with psychoanalysis.' This applies to both parties and explains how the analyst can 'stand it' – stand the turbulence. The modifying of anxiety is not entirely the responsibility of the analyst but rests on security provided by the psychoanalytic setting (though Bion does not use the word 'setting' much, just as he prefers not to use 'transference'). A mind-scene is created like a play in a theatre, in which the germ of an idea may be noticed and held for observation by the protagonists. And he is emphatic that the idea is 'born' of the *relationship* not either party alone.

But although there are two main protagonists (two bodies in the room), there are actually more 'shadowy' objects in the psychic setting. Bion insists there are always 'at least' three parties in the analytic setup – to include the third one that is observing or analysing the analyst. Prompted by Martha Harris in a seminar at the Tavistock to expand on what was meant by 'at least' three parties, it became clearer that the 'internal objects' operating in the consulting room belong not to one person but rather to the psychoanalytic pair. Later Donald Meltzer was to describe psychoanalysis as a 'conversation between internal objects.' This is slightly different from intersubjectivity: it is a conversation between the most advanced and thoughtful parts of each person, who remain separate, yet communicate across a caesura which displays both their differences and their essential identity, as at the caesura of birth. Thus the sense of at-one-ment or alignment with O (when it happens) represents an intersection not with a single person but with the analytic pair.

That is, when it is a true conversation and not (Bion warns) a false 'imitation' that looks like psychoanalysis but is really a basic assumption group, probably of the dependent or pairing type, whose sense of security is based on 'being good' rather than on the aesthetic harmony of 'That is sooth; accept it.' There is a danger in misconstruing container–contained as this type of comfortable complacent mutual parasitism. Just as the psychoanalysis itself is the container for the encounter, so the patient's attacks will be made on the *link* between the analyst and the analysis. The analyst has no favoured access to omniscience; if he is lucky there may be a 'fringe benefit' of increased self-knowledge.

Observation and O

Bion often spoke about the curious nature of psychoanalysis in studying the mind by using the same instrument that is being studied: the observer–observed.
The mind being observed changes through the act of
observing. Observation is the key to the psychoanalytic
method, as it is to any art or science, and Bion emphasises
this increasingly. The psychoanalytic task is to look for
evidence of a potential idea that is trying to get through
the psychic atmosphere (and that may appear as a 'wild
idea'). It is an exhausting struggle since we humans are
barely beginning to learn how to receive ideas, which
are almost imperceptible to our undeveloped mental
apparatus, and we are constantly being obstructed by
what he calls the 'noise' of basic assumptions, theories,
and other stuff that obscures observation. For example,
by way of defence, when tired or perhaps pushed by the
patient, the analyst may get a 'rush of theories to the
head'. Such theories when new may have represented
genuine discoveries, but using them as part of a moral
system denudes their language and the original or 'basic'
or thing is lost to sight. He was suspicious even of the
terms transference and countertransference, feeling that
too much falsehood had accrued to them.

Bion often quoted Freud's quotation of Charcot
on the importance of observation; but he extended it
to include the use of imagination. According to Bion
psychoanalytic observation cannot take place without
the use of imagination and he encouraged analysts to
'speculate' and 'give your imagination an airing', for the
only 'facts' to be met in psychoanalysis are 'the facts of
feeling' and these cannot be apprehended sensuously as

the body can be by the physician, so they need to be imagined. Bion also liked Freud's definition of consciousness as 'an organ for the perception of psychic qualities', but added that it could be turned either outward (as in the daytime) or inward (at night, in dreams). This implies that the psychoanalytic session is itself a type of dream being surveyed by the organ of consciousness; for Bion differentiated between the dream that 'happened' last night when the patient was asleep, and that which is told or occurs during the session, which is the only real evidence available to the psychoanalytic pair.

Finally, Bion saw psychoanalysis itself as one of those wild ideas with an 'origin' somewhere in the roots of human history and culture, awaiting Freud's specific genius to catch it and give it earthly form: it is an art-science both modern and ancient: 'Who are our ancestors?' The idea of psychoanalysis aligns itself with the idea of an individual personality that is wondering how to become itself. When in a seminar someone declared that everyone should have 'the right to make up their own mind' Bion replied that it was 'a nice idea' but that unfortunately, we need to come to terms with the fact that 'our minds are made up for us by forces about which we know nothing'. And the matter is put even more succinctly by the heroine of his *Memoir of the Future* when she says: 'I don't make up my mind – I let my mind make *me* up.' The psychoanalytic task is no different from that of everyday life: it is to relinquish illusory omnipotence, and align oneself with reality (O), internal and external. We can only become ourselves through reality-testing, namely, learning from experience the difference between truth and lies.

Meg Harris Williams

Although Bion said he did not wish his personal language to become technical jargon it is difficult to follow his written works without having some kind of translation or interpretation of his terminology in mind. The following headings are those I have found useful when teaching. The list is divided into three sections:

    I: The growth of thoughts
    II: Enemies of growth
    III: The psychoanalyst at work

I *The growth of thoughts*

Aesthetic – mysterious indication of alignment with O (truth).
Alpha function = symbol-formation. Develops feelings into thoughts via unconscious reverie (the thought does not need to be verbalised). Digests emotional distress to create meaning.
Becoming (Platonic) *vs.* 'learning about' (or: knowing via introjection, *vs.* knowing about). Link with deity or O.

Caesuras and meetings: receiving-screen or obscuring-screen? (eg, birth and pre- or post-natal parts; psyche and soma; sleeping and waking states; conscious and unconscious).

Catastrophic change. Means death to the existing state of mind – its many 'rebirths' constitute the process of growth. Set in motion when different parts/feelings/vertices try to link up.

Common sense – senses congregate across barriers or caesuras and interpenetrate (Meltzer compares Sullivan's 'consensuality').

Container–contained necessary for growth: male-female symbols represent the fundamental linkage. Relevant to multiple spheres.

Curiosity (originally, Oedipus): necessity of epistemophilic instinct; equivalent to life-force. May show in 'repetition compulsion' in the sense that the Answer may still be open.

Endoskeleton – allows mind to expand as more thoughts are accommodated; contrasts with exoskeleton or shell (of basic assumptions, etc.).

Genomene – psychic counterpart of phenomene, the originating germ of a thought.

Growth *vs.* correctness – true ethics. Room for growth. Occurs through link with object (initially breast/ maternal reverie).

Knowing *vs.* knowing about. (Both needed: knowing about is not necessarily Negative Grid). Intimate knowing means 'becoming'. Religious and scientific vertices.

Psyche-lodgement. The germ of an idea lodges in the mind in the gaps between knowledge, provided the surface of the knowledge is not too 'smooth' (too closed-off).

Myth and metaphor for categorising emotional cruxes; characterised by 'invariance', the 'basic feature' of a situation that is recognisable as a constant, even when translated into different media. Some examples: Oedipus (curiosity); Helen of Troy (absolute beauty, not describable); Palinurus (hidden latent turbulence); spiral nebula in astronomy (break-through); Monet's poppy-field; the sculpture trapping light; mathematical 'conjugate complex' points; the Grid; polyvalency (chemical analogy) implies openness to linking; river Alpheus and tracking of the idea. Sometimes called 'transformations' from one mode of expression into another.

Learning from experience (knowing *vs.* knowing about) – being and becoming.

LHK (Love, Hate, Knowledge). Turbulent emotions held in dramatic tension = 'passion'. Awe or dread accompanies the K link, intimations of O (the unknown). (Meltzer develops as 'aesthetic conflict'.)

Mind – an apparatus for receiving and digesting thoughts, anticipated by the glandular system. A new evolutionary development for the mammal. Synonymous with 'personality' or 'self' and includes both pre- and post-natal aspects.

Negative capability (Keats) – capacity to tolerate uncertainty; results in 'language of achievement'.

O = ultimate reality (unknowable); godlike ineffable object; origin; breast-shape as in point and circle. In Kleinian terms, an extension of the idea of the restored mother. Not just containment but identification with an evolving mind – with capacities and functions of object (see Money-Kyrle). Nearest analogy is 'passionate love', the LHK tension.

Object: the growth-promoting object is the analysis, not the analyst (Meltzer clarifies: the psychoanalytic process as aesthetic object). Created by a link between the 'pair' modelled on container–contained and maternal reverie.

Preconception – awaits linking with an 'other' or external feature that matches/fulfils/completes it, resulting in a conception/thought. Can be mismatched with a memory.

Pre-natal and post-natal parts of self need to meet and communicate across the mental caesura left over from birth. This unconscious link can catch the germ of an idea and allow it to develop. Prenatal life features: body-ego, id, rhythm, sense of smell, also light and sound.

Projective identification can be primitive communication (basis of reverie) rather than evacuation or intrusion. (See Meltzer for clarified distinction between communicative and intrusive projective identification.) Must be understood as part of an oscillation between paranoid-schizoid and depressive orientations (Ps↔D).

Ps↔D in continuous oscillation constitutes mind's normal condition. On the spectrum between uncertainty (stressful, suffering state) and aesthetic (momentary) harmony.

Realisation – expresses an achieved link between internal and external reality, a preconception and something that matches, confirms, and develops it.

Reverie (initially via the thinking breast). Unconscious processing of projected feelings, as in mother–baby relationship; verbalisation not necessary.

Self = psyche *and* soma, post and pre-natal personalities.

Turbulence is hated by the self and unless curiosity is strong enough, will be avoided: 'Kill it or find out about it' (that is, investigate its source and origin via intent observation). Uncomfortable state that heralds the presence of an idea and potential catastrophic change, i.e. growth.

Vertices of art, science, religion (also others). Each have own truth: need to find a tension not too slack, not too taut. Polyvalency is open to linkage.

Wisdom – distinct from intelligence. Acquired when the mind learns from experience; can apply to any phase in life even prenatal.

II *Enemies of growth*

Attacks on linking (minus LHK) where 'link' may include speech itself or the psychoanalytic method.

Basic assumption mentality (three types: fight-flight,

pairing/messianic, dependency). Exists in everyone both in group life and internally. Contrasts with work-group. Mindless *vs.* thinking orientation.

Beta-elements and beta-screen: unprocessed by alpha-function so do not lead to transformation via reverie into thoughts. Sometimes refers to undigested sense-impressions; sometimes alpha-elements that have been reversed (the mind's rubbish, for excretion).

Bizarre elements – way of dismantling elements of thinking.

Envy is essentially of 'the growth-promoting objects' and entails retreat to minus K (envious breast removes the will to live – this is how it deals with fear of dying).

Frustration – can be evaded (anti-growth), or alternatively, modified (growth – via link to the object).

Intelligence *vs.* wisdom – knowledge 'too thick' for wisdom.

Lies – defence against glimpse of the truth, covering it over with a substitute invented by the self. Can be systematised into 'morality', a rigidification of basic assumptions.

Language of substitution *vs.* language of achievement. Invented by the self rather than learned by alignment with O.

Memory and desire (*vs.* 'remembering') interpose preconceived pictures of the state the person wishes to attain; so blocks evolution from within.

Mindlessness (Meltzer's term, originally 'protomental') refers to a non-mental level which exists in everyone including sophisticated adults; one direction taken is childhood autism.

Nameless dread (Meltzer's 'terror') is less of death than of madness, the delusional system.

Negative Grid – not developed by Bion but according to Meltzer would be drawn up from Column 2 (lies): all the anti-thinking forces.

Pain and pleasure – two sides of one spectrum. Evasion of pain contrasts with 'modification' by the object. 'Suffering' means tolerating the pain until it is understood (through alpha function).

Paramnesias (after Freud) fill space of our ignorance; theories 'rush to the head' when thinking is too stressful.

Preconception instead of finding a realisation, can mate with a memory to prevent catastrophic change, blocking reception of the new idea.

Protomental level – all non-thinking mentality (but not necessarily anti-thought).

Psychosis: may show evidence of primitive or thwarted undeveloped thought with glimpses of insight, turned awry.

III *The psychoanalyst at work*

Aesthetic: a feeling of harmony or rightness that indicates truth is present.

Aim to introduce the patient to himself – 'a marriage that will last as long as he lives'.

At-one-ment = in line with O (sometimes 'alignment'). Intersects with the psychoanalytic pair. (Dislikes term 'countertransference'.) Overtones of religious atonement (Kleinian reparation; depressive position).

Consciousness (after Freud) as organ of perception for psychic qualities (even at night, turned inward). A tool for focusing. Verbal formulation comes afterwards.

Container–contained: the personality has a container–contained relationship with psycho*analysis* (rather than analyst): mutual modifying, shift in values.

Facts of feeling – basis of method.

Interpretations: can be 'rush of theories to the head' or can be genuine attempt to formulate what is observed. Beware pseudo-knowledge.

Language of achievement – speaking truly rather than

speaking poetically. Although the definition is based on admiration for poets' foreshadowing of the future – embodying ideas realised only centuries later. Contrasts with 'language of substitution' (failure to observe truly what is going on – substituting jargon, familiar ideas etc). Analyst must evolve own mode of expression, authentic rather than poetic.

Observation – the key to the psychoanalytic method. Theories are worthless by comparison with present observed phenomena. How to translate into articulate speech.

Mind – that which is being observed and changes through the act of observing. 'Our minds are made up for us by forces about which we know nothing.' The individual mind is a group not a single entity.

Noise (of jargon, previous knowledge etc) interferes with observing or hearing the idea present in the session.

Ps↔D oscillates between patience (toleration of not-knowing) and security (momentary sense of truth and harmony).

Psychoanalysis: distinctive method for germinating thoughts via a work-group of two (or more, if you include the 'third party' etc). Both partners in 'the psychoanalytic pair' are supported by the method. Not immune from harm or danger.

Reality-testing: distinguishing between evasion and modification of pain requires reality-testing – what is true, what is a lie. Reality is internal as well as external.

Remembering is essential owing to links with primordial traces. Like Platonic remembering (*anamnesis*) a glimpse of reality brought into present moment. The opposite of memory and desire, which indulge preconceptions and block contact with present reality.

Reverie is based on mother–baby and container–contained; the analyst relies on the analytic setting to be the container.

Speculative imagination/reason. No progress without it, even in natural sciences – still more when dealing with 'facts of feeling'.

Third party in a psychoanalytic setup: the analyser of the analyst. 'At least' three psychic parties even if only two bodies in the room.

Underlying pattern emerges as a result of patient ('suffering') observation.

Work group – the basis for thinking (the mental level). Entails toleration of individuality and difference. Contrasts with basic assumption groups (the non-mental level of existence). Can capture and track ideas.